C-1163   CAREER EXAMINATION SERIES

This is your
PASSBOOK for...

Caseworker Trainee

Test Preparation Study Guide
Questions & Answers

COPYRIGHT NOTICE

This book is SOLELY intended for, is sold ONLY to, and its use is RESTRICTED to individual, bona fide applicants or candidates who qualify by virtue of having seriously filed applications for appropriate license, certificate, professional and/or promotional advancement, higher school matriculation, scholarship, or other legitimate requirements of education and/or governmental authorities.

This book is NOT intended for use, class instruction, tutoring, training, duplication, copying, reprinting, excerption, or adaptation, etc., by:

1) Other publishers
2) Proprietors and/or Instructors of "Coaching" and/or Preparatory Courses
3) Personnel and/or Training Divisions of commercial, industrial, and governmental organizations
4) Schools, colleges, or universities and/or their departments and staffs, including teachers and other personnel
5) Testing Agencies or Bureaus
6) Study groups which seek by the purchase of a single volume to copy and/or duplicate and/or adapt this material for use by the group as a whole without having purchased individual volumes for each of the members of the group
7) Et al.

Such persons would be in violation of appropriate Federal and State statutes.

PROVISION OF LICENSING AGREEMENTS – Recognized educational, commercial, industrial, and governmental institutions and organizations, and others legitimately engaged in educational pursuits, including training, testing, and measurement activities, may address request for a licensing agreement to the copyright owners, who will determine whether, and under what conditions, including fees and charges, the materials in this book may be used them. In other words, a licensing facility exists for the legitimate use of the material in this book on other than an individual basis. However, it is asseverated and affirmed here that the material in this book CANNOT be used without the receipt of the express permission of such a licensing agreement from the Publishers. Inquiries re licensing should be addressed to the company, attention rights and permissions department.

All rights reserved, including the right of reproduction in whole or in part, in any form or by any means, electronic or mechanical, including photocopying, recording, or by any information storage and retrieval system, without permission in writing from the Publisher.

Copyright © 2024 by
National Learning Corporation

212 Michael Drive, Syosset, NY 11791
(516) 921-8888 • www.passbooks.com
E-mail: info@passbooks.com

PUBLISHED IN THE UNITED STATES OF AMERICA

PASSBOOK® SERIES

THE *PASSBOOK® SERIES* has been created to prepare applicants and candidates for the ultimate academic battlefield – the examination room.

At some time in our lives, each and every one of us may be required to take an examination – for validation, matriculation, admission, qualification, registration, certification, or licensure.

Based on the assumption that every applicant or candidate has met the basic formal educational standards, has taken the required number of courses, and read the necessary texts, the *PASSBOOK® SERIES* furnishes the one special preparation which may assure passing with confidence, instead of failing with insecurity. Examination questions – together with answers – are furnished as the basic vehicle for study so that the mysteries of the examination and its compounding difficulties may be eliminated or diminished by a sure method.

This book is meant to help you pass your examination provided that you qualify and are serious in your objective.

The entire field is reviewed through the huge store of content information which is succinctly presented through a provocative and challenging approach – the question-and-answer method.

A climate of success is established by furnishing the correct answers at the end of each test.

You soon learn to recognize types of questions, forms of questions, and patterns of questioning. You may even begin to anticipate expected outcomes.

You perceive that many questions are repeated or adapted so that you can gain acute insights, which may enable you to score many sure points.

You learn how to confront new questions, or types of questions, and to attack them confidently and work out the correct answers.

You note objectives and emphases, and recognize pitfalls and dangers, so that you may make positive educational adjustments.

Moreover, you are kept fully informed in relation to new concepts, methods, practices, and directions in the field.

You discover that you are actually taking the examination all the time: you are preparing for the examination by "taking" an examination, not by reading extraneous and/or supererogatory textbooks.

In short, this PASSBOOK®, used directedly, should be an important factor in helping you to pass your test.

CASEWORKER TRAINEE

DUTIES

Performs entry-level professional social work for individuals and families while receiving continuous on-the-job training. Attends special training sessions and participates in conferences and regular staff meetings. Studies and reviews literature and other materials related to casework to systematically acquire essential knowledge of the profession. Reviews existing case records, researches the background of clients, interviews clients, assesses the need for services, provides counseling, and establishes and maintains contacts in the development of needed resources.

The work involves providing social work services for individuals and/or their families in order to assist them with their economic, emotional, social, and environmental difficulties. The work is carried out in a variety of service areas including foster care, adoption, general family, adult protective and child protective services, and services to the elderly in accordance with Federal, State, and local policies and procedures. Work is performed under general supervision.
A Caseworker Trainee does related work as required. Trainee appointments consist of a probationary period following which incumbents receiving satisfactory ratings qualify for advancement to the title of Caseworker without further examination.

SCOPE OF THE EXAMINATION

The written test will be designed to test for knowledge, skills and/or abilities in such areas as:

1. **Establishing and maintaining effective helping relationships in a social casework setting** - These questions test for an understanding of the factors contributing to the development and maintenance of productive client-worker relationships. You will be provided with descriptions of specific client-worker interactions and asked to select the appropriate responses. The questions cover such topics as confidentiality, time management, professional ethics and referral techniques.
2. **Interviewing (Caseworker)** - These questions test for an understanding of the principles and techniques of interviewing and their application to specific client-worker situations. You will be provided with a series of concrete interviewing situations for which you will be required to select an appropriate course of action based on an analysis of the situation, the application of the information provided and ramifications of various interviewing principles and strategies. You will also be asked questions about the interviewing process and various interviewing techniques.
3. **Preparing written material** - These questions test for the ability to present information clearly and accurately and to organize paragraphs logically and comprehensibly. For some questions, you will be given information in two or three sentences followed by four restatements of the information. You must then choose the best version. For other questions, you will be given paragraphs with their sentences out of order and then asked to choose from four suggestions the best order for the sentences.

HOW TO TAKE A TEST

I. YOU MUST PASS AN EXAMINATION

A. *WHAT EVERY CANDIDATE SHOULD KNOW*

Examination applicants often ask us for help in preparing for the written test. What can I study in advance? What kinds of questions will be asked? How will the test be given? How will the papers be graded?

As an applicant for a civil service examination, you may be wondering about some of these things. Our purpose here is to suggest effective methods of advance study and to describe civil service examinations.

Your chances for success on this examination can be increased if you know how to prepare. Those "pre-examination jitters" can be reduced if you know what to expect. You can even experience an adventure in good citizenship if you know why civil service exams are given.

B. *WHY ARE CIVIL SERVICE EXAMINATIONS GIVEN?*

Civil service examinations are important to you in two ways. As a citizen, you want public jobs filled by employees who know how to do their work. As a job seeker, you want a fair chance to compete for that job on an equal footing with other candidates. The best-known means of accomplishing this two-fold goal is the competitive examination.

Exams are widely publicized throughout the nation. They may be administered for jobs in federal, state, city, municipal, town or village governments or agencies.

Any citizen may apply, with some limitations, such as the age or residence of applicants. Your experience and education may be reviewed to see whether you meet the requirements for the particular examination. When these requirements exist, they are reasonable and applied consistently to all applicants. Thus, a competitive examination may cause you some uneasiness now, but it is your privilege and safeguard.

C. *HOW ARE CIVIL SERVICE EXAMS DEVELOPED?*

Examinations are carefully written by trained technicians who are specialists in the field known as "psychological measurement," in consultation with recognized authorities in the field of work that the test will cover. These experts recommend the subject matter areas or skills to be tested; only those knowledges or skills important to your success on the job are included. The most reliable books and source materials available are used as references. Together, the experts and technicians judge the difficulty level of the questions.

Test technicians know how to phrase questions so that the problem is clearly stated. Their ethics do not permit "trick" or "catch" questions. Questions may have been tried out on sample groups, or subjected to statistical analysis, to determine their usefulness.

Written tests are often used in combination with performance tests, ratings of training and experience, and oral interviews. All of these measures combine to form the best-known means of finding the right person for the right job.

II. HOW TO PASS THE WRITTEN TEST

A. NATURE OF THE EXAMINATION

To prepare intelligently for civil service examinations, you should know how they differ from school examinations you have taken. In school you were assigned certain definite pages to read or subjects to cover. The examination questions were quite detailed and usually emphasized memory. Civil service exams, on the other hand, try to discover your present ability to perform the duties of a position, plus your potentiality to learn these duties. In other words, a civil service exam attempts to predict how successful you will be. Questions cover such a broad area that they cannot be as minute and detailed as school exam questions.

In the public service similar kinds of work, or positions, are grouped together in one "class." This process is known as *position-classification*. All the positions in a class are paid according to the salary range for that class. One class title covers all of these positions, and they are all tested by the same examination.

B. FOUR BASIC STEPS

1) Study the announcement

How, then, can you know what subjects to study? Our best answer is: "Learn as much as possible about the class of positions for which you've applied." The exam will test the knowledge, skills and abilities needed to do the work.

Your most valuable source of information about the position you want is the official exam announcement. This announcement lists the training and experience qualifications. Check these standards and apply only if you come reasonably close to meeting them.

The brief description of the position in the examination announcement offers some clues to the subjects which will be tested. Think about the job itself. Review the duties in your mind. Can you perform them, or are there some in which you are rusty? Fill in the blank spots in your preparation.

Many jurisdictions preview the written test in the exam announcement by including a section called "Knowledge and Abilities Required," "Scope of the Examination," or some similar heading. Here you will find out specifically what fields will be tested.

2) Review your own background

Once you learn in general what the position is all about, and what you need to know to do the work, ask yourself which subjects you already know fairly well and which need improvement. You may wonder whether to concentrate on improving your strong areas or on building some background in your fields of weakness. When the announcement has specified "some knowledge" or "considerable knowledge," or has used adjectives like "beginning principles of..." or "advanced ... methods," you can get a clue as to the number and difficulty of questions to be asked in any given field. More questions, and hence broader coverage, would be included for those subjects which are more important in the work. Now weigh your strengths and weaknesses against the job requirements and prepare accordingly.

3) Determine the level of the position

Another way to tell how intensively you should prepare is to understand the level of the job for which you are applying. Is it the entering level? In other words, is this the position in which beginners in a field of work are hired? Or is it an intermediate or advanced level? Sometimes this is indicated by such words as "Junior" or "Senior" in the class title. Other jurisdictions use Roman numerals to designate the level – Clerk I, Clerk II, for example. The word "Supervisor" sometimes appears in the title. If the level is not indicated by the title, check the description of duties. Will you be working under very close supervision, or will you have responsibility for independent decisions in this work?

4) Choose appropriate study materials

Now that you know the subjects to be examined and the relative amount of each subject to be covered, you can choose suitable study materials. For beginning level jobs, or even advanced ones, if you have a pronounced weakness in some aspect of your training, read a modern, standard textbook in that field. Be sure it is up to date and has general coverage. Such books are normally available at your library, and the librarian will be glad to help you locate one. For entry-level positions, questions of appropriate difficulty are chosen – neither highly advanced questions, nor those too simple. Such questions require careful thought but not advanced training.

If the position for which you are applying is technical or advanced, you will read more advanced, specialized material. If you are already familiar with the basic principles of your field, elementary textbooks would waste your time. Concentrate on advanced textbooks and technical periodicals. Think through the concepts and review difficult problems in your field.

These are all general sources. You can get more ideas on your own initiative, following these leads. For example, training manuals and publications of the government agency which employs workers in your field can be useful, particularly for technical and professional positions. A letter or visit to the government department involved may result in more specific study suggestions, and certainly will provide you with a more definite idea of the exact nature of the position you are seeking.

III. KINDS OF TESTS

Tests are used for purposes other than measuring knowledge and ability to perform specified duties. For some positions, it is equally important to test ability to make adjustments to new situations or to profit from training. In others, basic mental abilities not dependent on information are essential. Questions which test these things may not appear as pertinent to the duties of the position as those which test for knowledge and information. Yet they are often highly important parts of a fair examination. For very general questions, it is almost impossible to help you direct your study efforts. What we can do is to point out some of the more common of these general abilities needed in public service positions and describe some typical questions.

1) General information

Broad, general information has been found useful for predicting job success in some kinds of work. This is tested in a variety of ways, from vocabulary lists to questions about current events. Basic background in some field of work, such as sociology or economics, may be sampled in a group of questions. Often these are principles which have become familiar to most persons through exposure rather than through formal training. It is difficult to advise you how to study for these questions; being alert to the world around you is our best suggestion.

2) Verbal ability

An example of an ability needed in many positions is verbal or language ability. Verbal ability is, in brief, the ability to use and understand words. Vocabulary and grammar tests are typical measures of this ability. Reading comprehension or paragraph interpretation questions are common in many kinds of civil service tests. You are given a paragraph of written material and asked to find its central meaning.

3) **Numerical ability**
Number skills can be tested by the familiar arithmetic problem, by checking paired lists of numbers to see which are alike and which are different, or by interpreting charts and graphs. In the latter test, a graph may be printed in the test booklet which you are asked to use as the basis for answering questions.

4) **Observation**
A popular test for law-enforcement positions is the observation test. A picture is shown to you for several minutes, then taken away. Questions about the picture test your ability to observe both details and larger elements.

5) **Following directions**
In many positions in the public service, the employee must be able to carry out written instructions dependably and accurately. You may be given a chart with several columns, each column listing a variety of information. The questions require you to carry out directions involving the information given in the chart.

6) **Skills and aptitudes**
Performance tests effectively measure some manual skills and aptitudes. When the skill is one in which you are trained, such as typing or shorthand, you can practice. These tests are often very much like those given in business school or high school courses. For many of the other skills and aptitudes, however, no short-time preparation can be made. Skills and abilities natural to you or that you have developed throughout your lifetime are being tested.

Many of the general questions just described provide all the data needed to answer the questions and ask you to use your reasoning ability to find the answers. Your best preparation for these tests, as well as for tests of facts and ideas, is to be at your physical and mental best. You, no doubt, have your own methods of getting into an exam-taking mood and keeping "in shape." The next section lists some ideas on this subject.

IV. KINDS OF QUESTIONS

Only rarely is the "essay" question, which you answer in narrative form, used in civil service tests. Civil service tests are usually of the short-answer type. Full instructions for answering these questions will be given to you at the examination. But in case this is your first experience with short-answer questions and separate answer sheets, here is what you need to know:

1) Multiple-choice Questions
Most popular of the short-answer questions is the "multiple choice" or "best answer" question. It can be used, for example, to test for factual knowledge, ability to solve problems or judgment in meeting situations found at work.

A multiple-choice question is normally one of three types—
- It can begin with an incomplete statement followed by several possible endings. You are to find the one ending which *best* completes the statement, although some of the others may not be entirely wrong.
- It can also be a complete statement in the form of a question which is answered by choosing one of the statements listed.

- It can be in the form of a problem – again you select the best answer.

Here is an example of a multiple-choice question with a discussion which should give you some clues as to the method for choosing the right answer:

When an employee has a complaint about his assignment, the action which will *best* help him overcome his difficulty is to
- A. discuss his difficulty with his coworkers
- B. take the problem to the head of the organization
- C. take the problem to the person who gave him the assignment
- D. say nothing to anyone about his complaint

In answering this question, you should study each of the choices to find which is best. Consider choice "A" – Certainly an employee may discuss his complaint with fellow employees, but no change or improvement can result, and the complaint remains unresolved. Choice "B" is a poor choice since the head of the organization probably does not know what assignment you have been given, and taking your problem to him is known as "going over the head" of the supervisor. The supervisor, or person who made the assignment, is the person who can clarify it or correct any injustice. Choice "C" is, therefore, correct. To say nothing, as in choice "D," is unwise. Supervisors have and interest in knowing the problems employees are facing, and the employee is seeking a solution to his problem.

2) True/False Questions

The "true/false" or "right/wrong" form of question is sometimes used. Here a complete statement is given. Your job is to decide whether the statement is right or wrong.

SAMPLE: A roaming cell-phone call to a nearby city costs less than a non-roaming call to a distant city.

This statement is wrong, or false, since roaming calls are more expensive.

This is not a complete list of all possible question forms, although most of the others are variations of these common types. You will always get complete directions for answering questions. Be sure you understand *how* to mark your answers – ask questions until you do.

V. RECORDING YOUR ANSWERS

Computer terminals are used more and more today for many different kinds of exams.

For an examination with very few applicants, you may be told to record your answers in the test booklet itself. Separate answer sheets are much more common. If this separate answer sheet is to be scored by machine – and this is often the case – it is highly important that you mark your answers correctly in order to get credit.

An electronic scoring machine is often used in civil service offices because of the speed with which papers can be scored. Machine-scored answer sheets must be marked with a pencil, which will be given to you. This pencil has a high graphite content which responds to the electronic scoring machine. As a matter of fact, stray dots may register as answers, so do not let your pencil rest on the answer sheet while you are pondering the correct answer. Also, if your pencil lead breaks or is otherwise defective, ask for another.

Since the answer sheet will be dropped in a slot in the scoring machine, be careful not to bend the corners or get the paper crumpled.

The answer sheet normally has five vertical columns of numbers, with 30 numbers to a column. These numbers correspond to the question numbers in your test booklet. After each number, going across the page are four or five pairs of dotted lines. These short dotted lines have small letters or numbers above them. The first two pairs may also have a "T" or "F" above the letters. This indicates that the first two pairs only are to be used if the questions are of the true-false type. If the questions are multiple choice, disregard the "T" and "F" and pay attention only to the small letters or numbers.

Answer your questions in the manner of the sample that follows:

32. The largest city in the United States is
    A. Washington, D.C.
    B. New York City
    C. Chicago
    D. Detroit
    E. San Francisco

1) Choose the answer you think is best. (New York City is the largest, so "B" is correct.)
2) Find the row of dotted lines numbered the same as the question you are answering. (Find row number 32)
3) Find the pair of dotted lines corresponding to the answer. (Find the pair of lines under the mark "B.")
4) Make a solid black mark between the dotted lines.

VI. BEFORE THE TEST

Common sense will help you find procedures to follow to get ready for an examination. Too many of us, however, overlook these sensible measures. Indeed, nervousness and fatigue have been found to be the most serious reasons why applicants fail to do their best on civil service tests. Here is a list of reminders:

- Begin your preparation early – Don't wait until the last minute to go scurrying around for books and materials or to find out what the position is all about.
- Prepare continuously – An hour a night for a week is better than an all-night cram session. This has been definitely established. What is more, a night a week for a month will return better dividends than crowding your study into a shorter period of time.
- Locate the place of the exam – You have been sent a notice telling you when and where to report for the examination. If the location is in a different town or otherwise unfamiliar to you, it would be well to inquire the best route and learn something about the building.
- Relax the night before the test – Allow your mind to rest. Do not study at all that night. Plan some mild recreation or diversion; then go to bed early and get a good night's sleep.
- Get up early enough to make a leisurely trip to the place for the test – This way unforeseen events, traffic snarls, unfamiliar buildings, etc. will not upset you.
- Dress comfortably – A written test is not a fashion show. You will be known by number and not by name, so wear something comfortable.

- Leave excess paraphernalia at home – Shopping bags and odd bundles will get in your way. You need bring only the items mentioned in the official notice you received; usually everything you need is provided. Do not bring reference books to the exam. They will only confuse those last minutes and be taken away from you when in the test room.
- Arrive somewhat ahead of time – If because of transportation schedules you must get there very early, bring a newspaper or magazine to take your mind off yourself while waiting.
- Locate the examination room – When you have found the proper room, you will be directed to the seat or part of the room where you will sit. Sometimes you are given a sheet of instructions to read while you are waiting. Do not fill out any forms until you are told to do so; just read them and be prepared.
- Relax and prepare to listen to the instructions
- If you have any physical problem that may keep you from doing your best, be sure to tell the test administrator. If you are sick or in poor health, you really cannot do your best on the exam. You can come back and take the test some other time.

VII. AT THE TEST

The day of the test is here and you have the test booklet in your hand. The temptation to get going is very strong. Caution! There is more to success than knowing the right answers. You must know how to identify your papers and understand variations in the type of short-answer question used in this particular examination. Follow these suggestions for maximum results from your efforts:

1) Cooperate with the monitor

The test administrator has a duty to create a situation in which you can be as much at ease as possible. He will give instructions, tell you when to begin, check to see that you are marking your answer sheet correctly, and so on. He is not there to guard you, although he will see that your competitors do not take unfair advantage. He wants to help you do your best.

2) Listen to all instructions

Don't jump the gun! Wait until you understand all directions. In most civil service tests you get more time than you need to answer the questions. So don't be in a hurry. Read each word of instructions until you clearly understand the meaning. Study the examples, listen to all announcements and follow directions. Ask questions if you do not understand what to do.

3) Identify your papers

Civil service exams are usually identified by number only. You will be assigned a number; you must not put your name on your test papers. Be sure to copy your number correctly. Since more than one exam may be given, copy your exact examination title.

4) Plan your time

Unless you are told that a test is a "speed" or "rate of work" test, speed itself is usually not important. Time enough to answer all the questions will be provided, but this does not mean that you have all day. An overall time limit has been set. Divide the total time (in minutes) by the number of questions to determine the approximate time you have for each question.

5) Do not linger over difficult questions

If you come across a difficult question, mark it with a paper clip (useful to have along) and come back to it when you have been through the booklet. One caution if you do this – be sure to skip a number on your answer sheet as well. Check often to be sure that you have not lost your place and that you are marking in the row numbered the same as the question you are answering.

6) Read the questions

Be sure you know what the question asks! Many capable people are unsuccessful because they failed to *read* the questions correctly.

7) Answer all questions

Unless you have been instructed that a penalty will be deducted for incorrect answers, it is better to guess than to omit a question.

8) Speed tests

It is often better NOT to guess on speed tests. It has been found that on timed tests people are tempted to spend the last few seconds before time is called in marking answers at random – without even reading them – in the hope of picking up a few extra points. To discourage this practice, the instructions may warn you that your score will be "corrected" for guessing. That is, a penalty will be applied. The incorrect answers will be deducted from the correct ones, or some other penalty formula will be used.

9) Review your answers

If you finish before time is called, go back to the questions you guessed or omitted to give them further thought. Review other answers if you have time.

10) Return your test materials

If you are ready to leave before others have finished or time is called, take ALL your materials to the monitor and leave quietly. Never take any test material with you. The monitor can discover whose papers are not complete, and taking a test booklet may be grounds for disqualification.

VIII. EXAMINATION TECHNIQUES

1) Read the general instructions carefully. These are usually printed on the first page of the exam booklet. As a rule, these instructions refer to the timing of the examination; the fact that you should not start work until the signal and must stop work at a signal, etc. If there are any *special* instructions, such as a choice of questions to be answered, make sure that you note this instruction carefully.

2) When you are ready to start work on the examination, that is as soon as the signal has been given, read the instructions to each question booklet, underline any key words or phrases, such as *least, best, outline, describe* and the like. In this way you will tend to answer as requested rather than discover on reviewing your paper that you *listed without describing*, that you selected the *worst* choice rather than the *best* choice, etc.

3) If the examination is of the objective or multiple-choice type – that is, each question will also give a series of possible answers: A, B, C or D, and you are called upon to select the best answer and write the letter next to that answer on your answer paper – it is advisable to start answering each question in turn. There may be anywhere from 50 to 100 such questions in the three or four hours allotted and you can see how much time would be taken if you read through all the questions before beginning to answer any. Furthermore, if you come across a question or group of questions which you know would be difficult to answer, it would undoubtedly affect your handling of all the other questions.

4) If the examination is of the essay type and contains but a few questions, it is a moot point as to whether you should read all the questions before starting to answer any one. Of course, if you are given a choice – say five out of seven and the like – then it is essential to read all the questions so you can eliminate the two that are most difficult. If, however, you are asked to answer all the questions, there may be danger in trying to answer the easiest one first because you may find that you will spend too much time on it. The best technique is to answer the first question, then proceed to the second, etc.

5) Time your answers. Before the exam begins, write down the time it started, then add the time allowed for the examination and write down the time it must be completed, then divide the time available somewhat as follows:
   - If 3-1/2 hours are allowed, that would be 210 minutes. If you have 80 objective-type questions, that would be an average of 2-1/2 minutes per question. Allow yourself no more than 2 minutes per question, or a total of 160 minutes, which will permit about 50 minutes to review.
   - If for the time allotment of 210 minutes there are 7 essay questions to answer, that would average about 30 minutes a question. Give yourself only 25 minutes per question so that you have about 35 minutes to review.

6) The most important instruction is to *read each question* and make sure you know what is wanted. The second most important instruction is to *time yourself properly* so that you answer every question. The third most important instruction is to *answer every question*. Guess if you have to but include something for each question. Remember that you will receive no credit for a blank and will probably receive some credit if you write something in answer to an essay question. If you guess a letter – say "B" for a multiple-choice question – you may have guessed right. If you leave a blank as an answer to a multiple-choice question, the examiners may respect your feelings but it will not add a point to your score. Some exams may penalize you for wrong answers, so in such cases *only*, you may not want to guess unless you have some basis for your answer.

7) Suggestions
   a. Objective-type questions
      1. Examine the question booklet for proper sequence of pages and questions
      2. Read all instructions carefully
      3. Skip any question which seems too difficult; return to it after all other questions have been answered
      4. Apportion your time properly; do not spend too much time on any single question or group of questions

5. Note and underline key words – *all, most, fewest, least, best, worst, same, opposite*, etc.
6. Pay particular attention to negatives
7. Note unusual option, e.g., unduly long, short, complex, different or similar in content to the body of the question
8. Observe the use of "hedging" words – *probably, may, most likely*, etc.
9. Make sure that your answer is put next to the same number as the question
10. Do not second-guess unless you have good reason to believe the second answer is definitely more correct
11. Cross out original answer if you decide another answer is more accurate; do not erase until you are ready to hand your paper in
12. Answer all questions; guess unless instructed otherwise
13. Leave time for review

b. Essay questions
   1. Read each question carefully
   2. Determine exactly what is wanted. Underline key words or phrases.
   3. Decide on outline or paragraph answer
   4. Include many different points and elements unless asked to develop any one or two points or elements
   5. Show impartiality by giving pros and cons unless directed to select one side only
   6. Make and write down any assumptions you find necessary to answer the questions
   7. Watch your English, grammar, punctuation and choice of words
   8. Time your answers; don't crowd material

8) Answering the essay question

Most essay questions can be answered by framing the specific response around several key words or ideas. Here are a few such key words or ideas:

M's: manpower, materials, methods, money, management
P's: purpose, program, policy, plan, procedure, practice, problems, pitfalls, personnel, public relations
   a. Six basic steps in handling problems:
      1. Preliminary plan and background development
      2. Collect information, data and facts
      3. Analyze and interpret information, data and facts
      4. Analyze and develop solutions as well as make recommendations
      5. Prepare report and sell recommendations
      6. Install recommendations and follow up effectiveness

   b. Pitfalls to avoid
      1. *Taking things for granted* – A statement of the situation does not necessarily imply that each of the elements is necessarily true; for example, a complaint may be invalid and biased so that all that can be taken for granted is that a complaint has been registered

2. *Considering only one side of a situation* – Wherever possible, indicate several alternatives and then point out the reasons you selected the best one
3. *Failing to indicate follow up* – Whenever your answer indicates action on your part, make certain that you will take proper follow-up action to see how successful your recommendations, procedures or actions turn out to be
4. *Taking too long in answering any single question* – Remember to time your answers properly

IX. AFTER THE TEST

Scoring procedures differ in detail among civil service jurisdictions although the general principles are the same. Whether the papers are hand-scored or graded by machine we have described, they are nearly always graded by number. That is, the person who marks the paper knows only the number – never the name – of the applicant. Not until all the papers have been graded will they be matched with names. If other tests, such as training and experience or oral interview ratings have been given, scores will be combined. Different parts of the examination usually have different weights. For example, the written test might count 60 percent of the final grade, and a rating of training and experience 40 percent. In many jurisdictions, veterans will have a certain number of points added to their grades.

After the final grade has been determined, the names are placed in grade order and an eligible list is established. There are various methods for resolving ties between those who get the same final grade – probably the most common is to place first the name of the person whose application was received first. Job offers are made from the eligible list in the order the names appear on it. You will be notified of your grade and your rank as soon as all these computations have been made. This will be done as rapidly as possible.

People who are found to meet the requirements in the announcement are called "eligibles." Their names are put on a list of eligible candidates. An eligible's chances of getting a job depend on how high he stands on this list and how fast agencies are filling jobs from the list.

When a job is to be filled from a list of eligibles, the agency asks for the names of people on the list of eligibles for that job. When the civil service commission receives this request, it sends to the agency the names of the three people highest on this list. Or, if the job to be filled has specialized requirements, the office sends the agency the names of the top three persons who meet these requirements from the general list.

The appointing officer makes a choice from among the three people whose names were sent to him. If the selected person accepts the appointment, the names of the others are put back on the list to be considered for future openings.

That is the rule in hiring from all kinds of eligible lists, whether they are for typist, carpenter, chemist, or something else. For every vacancy, the appointing officer has his choice of any one of the top three eligibles on the list. This explains why the person whose name is on top of the list sometimes does not get an appointment when some of the persons lower on the list do. If the appointing officer chooses the second or third eligible, the No. 1 eligible does not get a job at once, but stays on the list until he is appointed or the list is terminated.

X. HOW TO PASS THE INTERVIEW TEST

The examination for which you applied requires an oral interview test. You have already taken the written test and you are now being called for the interview test – the final part of the formal examination.

You may think that it is not possible to prepare for an interview test and that there are no procedures to follow during an interview. Our purpose is to point out some things you can do in advance that will help you and some good rules to follow and pitfalls to avoid while you are being interviewed.

What is an interview supposed to test?

The written examination is designed to test the technical knowledge and competence of the candidate; the oral is designed to evaluate intangible qualities, not readily measured otherwise, and to establish a list showing the relative fitness of each candidate – as measured against his competitors – for the position sought. Scoring is not on the basis of "right" and "wrong," but on a sliding scale of values ranging from "not passable" to "outstanding." As a matter of fact, it is possible to achieve a relatively low score without a single "incorrect" answer because of evident weakness in the qualities being measured.

Occasionally, an examination may consist entirely of an oral test – either an individual or a group oral. In such cases, information is sought concerning the technical knowledges and abilities of the candidate, since there has been no written examination for this purpose. More commonly, however, an oral test is used to supplement a written examination.

Who conducts interviews?

The composition of oral boards varies among different jurisdictions. In nearly all, a representative of the personnel department serves as chairman. One of the members of the board may be a representative of the department in which the candidate would work. In some cases, "outside experts" are used, and, frequently, a businessman or some other representative of the general public is asked to serve. Labor and management or other special groups may be represented. The aim is to secure the services of experts in the appropriate field.

However the board is composed, it is a good idea (and not at all improper or unethical) to ascertain in advance of the interview who the members are and what groups they represent. When you are introduced to them, you will have some idea of their backgrounds and interests, and at least you will not stutter and stammer over their names.

What should be done before the interview?

While knowledge about the board members is useful and takes some of the surprise element out of the interview, there is other preparation which is more substantive. It *is* possible to prepare for an oral interview – in several ways:

1) Keep a copy of your application and review it carefully before the interview

This may be the only document before the oral board, and the starting point of the interview. Know what education and experience you have listed there, and the sequence and dates of all of it. Sometimes the board will ask you to review the highlights of your experience for them; you should not have to hem and haw doing it.

2) Study the class specification and the examination announcement

Usually, the oral board has one or both of these to guide them. The qualities, characteristics or knowledges required by the position sought are stated in these documents. They offer valuable clues as to the nature of the oral interview. For example, if the job involves supervisory responsibilities, the announcement will usually indicate that knowledge of modern supervisory methods and the qualifications of the candidate as a supervisor will be tested. If so, you can expect such questions, frequently in the form of a hypothetical situation which you are expected to solve. NEVER go into an oral without knowledge of the duties and responsibilities of the job you seek.

3) Think through each qualification required

Try to visualize the kind of questions you would ask if you were a board member. How well could you answer them? Try especially to appraise your own knowledge and background in each area, *measured against the job sought*, and identify any areas in which you are weak. Be critical and realistic – do not flatter yourself.

4) Do some general reading in areas in which you feel you may be weak

For example, if the job involves supervision and your past experience has NOT, some general reading in supervisory methods and practices, particularly in the field of human relations, might be useful. Do NOT study agency procedures or detailed manuals. The oral board will be testing your understanding and capacity, not your memory.

5) Get a good night's sleep and watch your general health and mental attitude

You will want a clear head at the interview. Take care of a cold or any other minor ailment, and of course, no hangovers.

What should be done on the day of the interview?

Now comes the day of the interview itself. Give yourself plenty of time to get there. Plan to arrive somewhat ahead of the scheduled time, particularly if your appointment is in the fore part of the day. If a previous candidate fails to appear, the board might be ready for you a bit early. By early afternoon an oral board is almost invariably behind schedule if there are many candidates, and you may have to wait. Take along a book or magazine to read, or your application to review, but leave any extraneous material in the waiting room when you go in for your interview. In any event, relax and compose yourself.

The matter of dress is important. The board is forming impressions about you – from your experience, your manners, your attitude, and your appearance. Give your personal appearance careful attention. Dress your best, but not your flashiest. Choose conservative, appropriate clothing, and be sure it is immaculate. This is a business interview, and your appearance should indicate that you regard it as such. Besides, being well groomed and properly dressed will help boost your confidence.

Sooner or later, someone will call your name and escort you into the interview room. *This is it.* From here on you are on your own. It is too late for any more preparation. But remember, you asked for this opportunity to prove your fitness, and you are here because your request was granted.

What happens when you go in?

The usual sequence of events will be as follows: The clerk (who is often the board stenographer) will introduce you to the chairman of the oral board, who will introduce you to the other members of the board. Acknowledge the introductions before you sit down. Do not be surprised if you find a microphone facing you or a stenotypist sitting by. Oral interviews are usually recorded in the event of an appeal or other review.

Usually the chairman of the board will open the interview by reviewing the highlights of your education and work experience from your application – primarily for the benefit of the other members of the board, as well as to get the material into the record. Do not interrupt or comment unless there is an error or significant misinterpretation; if that is the case, do not hesitate. But do not quibble about insignificant matters. Also, he will usually ask you some question about your education, experience or your present job – partly to get you to start talking and to establish the interviewing "rapport." He may start the actual questioning, or turn it over to one of the other members. Frequently, each member undertakes the questioning on a particular area, one in which he is perhaps most competent, so you can expect each member to participate in the examination. Because time is limited, you may also expect some rather abrupt switches in the direction the questioning takes, so do not be upset by it. Normally, a board member will not pursue a single line of questioning unless he discovers a particular strength or weakness.

After each member has participated, the chairman will usually ask whether any member has any further questions, then will ask you if you have anything you wish to add. Unless you are expecting this question, it may floor you. Worse, it may start you off on an extended, extemporaneous speech. The board is not usually seeking more information. The question is principally to offer you a last opportunity to present further qualifications or to indicate that you have nothing to add. So, if you feel that a significant qualification or characteristic has been overlooked, it is proper to point it out in a sentence or so. Do not compliment the board on the thoroughness of their examination – they have been sketchy, and you know it. If you wish, merely say, "No thank you, I have nothing further to add." This is a point where you can "talk yourself out" of a good impression or fail to present an important bit of information. Remember, *you close the interview yourself.*

The chairman will then say, "That is all, Mr. _____, thank you." Do not be startled; the interview is over, and quicker than you think. Thank him, gather your belongings and take your leave. Save your sigh of relief for the other side of the door.

How to put your best foot forward

Throughout this entire process, you may feel that the board individually and collectively is trying to pierce your defenses, seek out your hidden weaknesses and embarrass and confuse you. Actually, this is not true. They are obliged to make an appraisal of your qualifications for the job you are seeking, and they want to see you in your best light. Remember, they must interview all candidates and a non-cooperative candidate may become a failure in spite of their best efforts to bring out his qualifications. Here are 15 suggestions that will help you:

1) Be natural – Keep your attitude confident, not cocky

If you are not confident that you can do the job, do not expect the board to be. Do not apologize for your weaknesses, try to bring out your strong points. The board is interested in a positive, not negative, presentation. Cockiness will antagonize any board member and make him wonder if you are covering up a weakness by a false show of strength.

2) Get comfortable, but don't lounge or sprawl

Sit erectly but not stiffly. A careless posture may lead the board to conclude that you are careless in other things, or at least that you are not impressed by the importance of the occasion. Either conclusion is natural, even if incorrect. Do not fuss with your clothing, a pencil or an ashtray. Your hands may occasionally be useful to emphasize a point; do not let them become a point of distraction.

3) Do not wisecrack or make small talk

This is a serious situation, and your attitude should show that you consider it as such. Further, the time of the board is limited – they do not want to waste it, and neither should you.

4) Do not exaggerate your experience or abilities
In the first place, from information in the application or other interviews and sources, the board may know more about you than you think. Secondly, you probably will not get away with it. An experienced board is rather adept at spotting such a situation, so do not take the chance.

5) If you know a board member, do not make a point of it, yet do not hide it
Certainly you are not fooling him, and probably not the other members of the board. Do not try to take advantage of your acquaintanceship – it will probably do you little good.

6) Do not dominate the interview
Let the board do that. They will give you the clues – do not assume that you have to do all the talking. Realize that the board has a number of questions to ask you, and do not try to take up all the interview time by showing off your extensive knowledge of the answer to the first one.

7) Be attentive
You only have 20 minutes or so, and you should keep your attention at its sharpest throughout. When a member is addressing a problem or question to you, give him your undivided attention. Address your reply principally to him, but do not exclude the other board members.

8) Do not interrupt
A board member may be stating a problem for you to analyze. He will ask you a question when the time comes. Let him state the problem, and wait for the question.

9) Make sure you understand the question
Do not try to answer until you are sure what the question is. If it is not clear, restate it in your own words or ask the board member to clarify it for you. However, do not haggle about minor elements.

10) Reply promptly but not hastily
A common entry on oral board rating sheets is "candidate responded readily," or "candidate hesitated in replies." Respond as promptly and quickly as you can, but do not jump to a hasty, ill-considered answer.

11) Do not be peremptory in your answers
A brief answer is proper – but do not fire your answer back. That is a losing game from your point of view. The board member can probably ask questions much faster than you can answer them.

12) Do not try to create the answer you think the board member wants
He is interested in what kind of mind you have and how it works – not in playing games. Furthermore, he can usually spot this practice and will actually grade you down on it.

13) Do not switch sides in your reply merely to agree with a board member
Frequently, a member will take a contrary position merely to draw you out and to see if you are willing and able to defend your point of view. Do not start a debate, yet do not surrender a good position. If a position is worth taking, it is worth defending.

14) Do not be afraid to admit an error in judgment if you are shown to be wrong
The board knows that you are forced to reply without any opportunity for careful consideration. Your answer may be demonstrably wrong. If so, admit it and get on with the interview.

15) Do not dwell at length on your present job
The opening question may relate to your present assignment. Answer the question but do not go into an extended discussion. You are being examined for a *new* job, not your present one. As a matter of fact, try to phrase ALL your answers in terms of the job for which you are being examined.

Basis of Rating
Probably you will forget most of these "do's" and "don'ts" when you walk into the oral interview room. Even remembering them all will not ensure you a passing grade. Perhaps you did not have the qualifications in the first place. But remembering them will help you to put your best foot forward, without treading on the toes of the board members.

Rumor and popular opinion to the contrary notwithstanding, an oral board wants you to make the best appearance possible. They know you are under pressure – but they also want to see how you respond to it as a guide to what your reaction would be under the pressures of the job you seek. They will be influenced by the degree of poise you display, the personal traits you show and the manner in which you respond.

ABOUT THIS BOOK

This book contains tests divided into Examination Sections. Go through each test, answering every question in the margin. We have also attached a sample answer sheet at the back of the book that can be removed and used. At the end of each test look at the answer key and check your answers. On the ones you got wrong, look at the right answer choice and learn. Do not fill in the answers first. Do not memorize the questions and answers, but understand the answer and principles involved. On your test, the questions will likely be different from the samples. Questions are changed and new ones added. If you understand these past questions you should have success with any changes that arise. Tests may consist of several types of questions. We have additional books on each subject should more study be advisable or necessary for you. Finally, the more you study, the better prepared you will be. This book is intended to be the last thing you study before you walk into the examination room. Prior study of relevant texts is also recommended. NLC publishes some of these in our Fundamental Series. Knowledge and good sense are important factors in passing your exam. Good luck also helps. So now study this Passbook, absorb the material contained within and take that knowledge into the examination. Then do your best to pass that exam.

EXAMINATION SECTION

EXAMINATION SECTION
TEST 1

DIRECTIONS: Each question or incomplete statement is followed by several suggested answers or completions. Select the one that BEST answers the question or completes the statement. *PRINT THE LETTER OF THE CORRECT ANSWER IN THE SPACE AT THE RIGHT.*

1. Local responsibility for the relief of economic need long having been recognized as inadequate, the state and federal governments have established schemes of *categorical* assistance and social insurance.
   In the preceding sentence, the italicized word means MOST NEARLY
      A. conditional   B. economic   C. pecuniary   D. classified

   1.____

2. When a person *vicariously* lives out his own problems in novels and plays, he is engaging in an experience that is, in terms of the italicized word in this sentence
      A. dynamic   B. monastic   C. substituted   D. dignified

   2.____

3. The Alcoholics Anonymous program, which in essence amounts to a *therapeutic* procedure, is codified into twelve steps.
   The italicized word in the preceding sentence means MOST NEARLY
      A. compensatory   B. curative   C. sequential   D. volitional

   3.____

4. The case of Mary Smith who ordered her husband out of the house and begged his pardon before he could leave, if accepted as characteristic behavior on the part of this woman, is BEST considered as an illustration of
      A. ambivalence   B. compensation
      C. retrogression   D. frustration

   4.____

5. To say that the Community Chest movement seems to have been *indigenous* to the North American continent describes this movement, in terms of the italicized word in this sentence MOST NEARLY as
      A. imported   B. essential   C. native   D. homogeneous

   5.____

6. There should be no *opprobrium* attached to the term "second-hand housing" since every house is second-hand after the first occupancy.
   The italicized word in the preceding sentence means MOST NEARLY
      A. stigma   B. honor   C. rank   D. credit

   6.____

7. Clinics are now seeing many people who complain of seriously disturbed feelings and other symptoms relating to *traumatic* war experiences.
   In the preceding sentence, the italicized word means MOST NEARLY
      A. recent   B. worldwide   C. prodigious   D. shocking

   7.____

8. The nature of the *pathology* underlying the compulsion is obscure.
   In the preceding sentence, the italicized word means MOST NEARLY
      A. drive   B. disease   C. deterioration   D. development

8.____

9. If the interests of a social welfare agency are concerned with bringing opportunities for self-help to underprivileged *ethnic* groups, its activities involve MOST NEARLY, in terms of the italicized word in this sentence,
      A. racial factors   B. minority units
      C. religious affiliations   D. economic conditions

9.____

10. Increased facilities for medical care (though interrupted to some extent by the *exigencies* of wartime) will safeguard the health of many children who in previous generations would have been doomed to an early death or to physical disability.
    In the above sentence the MOST NEARLY CORRECT equivalent of the italicized word is
       A. obstacles   B. occurrences   C. extenuations   D. exactions

10.____

11. The name of Sanford Bate would be associated by a well-read social service worker with the book entitled
       A. THE FAMILY   B. SOCIAL CHANGE
       C. PRISONS AND BEYOND   D. HULL HOUSE

11.____

Questions 12-16.

DIRECTIONS: In Questions 12 through 16 below, Column I consists of items referring to certain characteristics of areas usually found to exist in most American cities. Column II describes four sections into which the general sociological pattern of the modern city may be divided. Select the description in Column II to which the reference in Column I is MOST appropriate.

COLUMN I	COLUMN II	
12. The area in which a predominantly male resident population would probably be found.	A. Retail stores, eating establishments, motion picture theater, offices of professional people and business organizations	12.____
13. The area in which a *slum* would probably be located if it existed in this city.	B. Made-over private dwellings, rooming houses, cheap hotels pawnbrokers, wholesale business establishments	13.____
14. The area in which the most prominent citizens of the community would probably be found living	C. Less crowding than in above area, more modern houses, fewer children, wives not generally gainfully employed	14.____
15. The area likely to contain the sparsest resident population	D. Fashionable suburbs homes of professional and business leaders, relative cleanliness and modernity	15.____
16. The area likely to be inhabited by middle-class families		16.____

3 (#1)

17. To the social service worker who has maintained an interest in the field of psychiatry, THE NEUROTIC PERSONALITY OF OUR TIME would suggest
    A. Margaret Mead
    B. R.S. Lynd and H.M. Lynd
    C. Karen Horney
    D. Ruth Benedict

17._____

18. The conscientious social service worker is interested in the provisions of the Wagner-Ellender-Taft bill because the subject of this Congressional legislation was
    A. rent control
    B. housing
    C. tax reduction
    D. health insurance

18._____

19. Of the following, the name MOST closely identified with developments leading to the enactment of the Social Security Act was
    A. Harry Hopkins
    B. William Beveridge
    C. Herbert C. Hoover
    D. Arthur J. Altmeyer

19._____

20. The federal government will grant reimbursement under the Social Security Act to states for certain categories of assistance, provided the state law is in conformance with the requirements of the Act.
    One of the following requirements which is enforced by the federal government is that
    A. citizenship must be required as a condition of eligibility
    B. some residence requirement must be included
    C. payment to the client must be *money payment*
    D. some exemptions from merit system operation must be provided

20._____

21. Of the following social services administered by public agencies, the one administered by the federal government is
    A. unemployment compensation
    B. old age and survivors insurance
    C. vocational rehabilitation for civilians
    D. civilian war assistance

21._____

22. Most old age assistance program have been limited in general to the financial and physical needs of the aged because
    A. it is impossible to determine their other needs with any degree of practicality
    B. social agencies are unwilling to enlarge their responsibilities for the care of the aged
    C. old people are not interested in social participation
    D. public relief administrators have not been given the means to undertake more augmented programs

22._____

23. Of the qualifications and procedures connected with the method under which an insured individual may receive old age and survivors insurance, three are given below.

23._____

The statement which is NOT among these qualifications or procedures is that the individual
- A. must have been employed in covered employment for certain specified periods of time
- B. must have attained the age of 65
- C. has his primary benefit amounts computed in relation to his record earnings in covered employment
- D. is disqualified to receive old-age and survivors insurance benefits for any month in which he had an earned income of $100 or less

24. One of the requirements regarding an institution in which the Department of Social Service may place a neglected child is that the institution must
    - A. have been certified by the State Board of Social Welfare
    - B. be operated on a non-sectarian basis
    - C. have been incorporated for a period of not less than three years
    - D. be situated within the geographical limits of the city

25. With respect to destitute children placed out in institutions as public charges, the Commissioner of Social Services
    - A. may not deputize subordinates to make an investigation of such an institution except through the Department of Licenses
    - B. may reimburse such an institution for any expense, other than salaries, actually incurred in the placing out
    - C. may not authorize an institution to which a child has been committed to place such a child in a family
    - D. may transfer a child from one institution to another, except when either institution is governed by persons professing the same religious faith as the parents of the child

26. George Bailey, who has been unable to earn a living because of a recent industrial accident, is referred to his nearest social services center and subsequently placed in an institution for rehabilitation and training so that he will become a permanent charge upon the public. Bailey has a son whom the social service reports as unwilling, though sufficiently able, to support his incapacitated father.
    If the Commissioner of Social Services wishes to compel Bailey's son to pay a reasonable charge for Bailey's care in the institution, he would apply for the necessary order to the
    - A. Family Court
    - B. Supreme Court
    - C. State Board of Social Services
    - D. Court of Appeals

27. Commitment by the Department of Social Services invariably implies that the parents
    - A. have maltreated the child
    - B. are unable to support the child
    - C. have, through voluntary agreement, given custody of the child to the Commissioner of Social Services
    - D. have given the child up for adoption

28. The service of the Department of Social Services which is financed jointly by the city, state, and federal governments is
    A. veterans assistance
    B. aid to dependent children
    C. home relief
    D. the cost of board in foster home care for children

28.____

29. The LEAST applicable of the following statements regarding unemployment compensation for workers in this state is
    A. the employer pays the total tax for unemployment compensation
    B. the maximum period of benefit payments is 26 weeks in any benefit year
    C. benefit payments are the same whether a person has been discharged from his job on account of retrenchment or is unemployed on account of illness
    D. employees of philanthropic and religious organizations are not included in coverage

29.____

30. Ten months ago, Mr. Johnson came to this city from Plattsburgh, New York, where he had lived for ten years. Unable to find work, he applies at your welfare center for assistance for himself and his family.
    As an acting intake interviewer, you should tell Mr. Johnson that
    A. he is ineligible for relief since his needs are the responsibility of another municipality
    B. he is ineligible for relief and should return to Plattsburgh because no jobs are available in this city
    C. he should wait two more months in order to attain the required year's settlement
    D. his application is acceptable and his eligibility on the basis of need will be determined

30.____

KEY (CORRECT ANSWERS)

1.	D	11.	C	21.	B
2.	C	12.	B	22.	D
3.	B	13.	B	23.	D
4.	A	14.	D	24.	A
5.	C	15.	A	25.	B
6.	A	16.	C	26.	A
7.	D	17.	C	27.	C
8.	B	18.	B	28.	B
9.	A	19.	A	29.	C
10.	D	20.	C	30.	D

TEST 2

DIRECTIONS: Each question or incomplete statement is followed by several suggested answers or completions. Select the one that BEST answers the question or completes the statement. *PRINT THE LETTER OF THE CORRECT ANSWER IN THE SPACE AT THE RIGHT.*

1. A war veteran in need of public assistance and care who applies for such relief in this city will be eligible to receive such help if he
   A. had been discharged from military service only under honorable conditions
   B. is a resident of this city on the date of application for public assistance
   C. has been a state resident for a period of one year or more
   D. was a resident of the city at the time he entered the military service

   1._____

2. Mrs. Doe was receiving aid to dependent children for the third year when, in the course of reinvestigation, the social service worker discovered that she had a part-time job and arranged to reduce her relief accordingly. Mrs. Doe objected to the reduction and, after discussing her case with the proper officials in the Department of Social Services, decided to file a final appeal from their decision.
   A social service worker aware of the proper procedure to be followed in this case would have advised Mrs. Doe that the highest authority to which she could appeal is the
   A. Social Security Administration
   B. State Charities Aid
   C. Commissioner of Social Services
   D. State Department of Social Welfare

   2._____

3. A social service worker receives complaints from neighbors that the three children of a certain relief family are being neglected by their parents to the point where their health and safety are endangered, and suggestions are made that the youngsters be separated from their negligent parents.
   Authority to order removal of the children from their home, if investigation substantiates these charges, is vested PRIMARILY in
   A. the Commissioner of Social Services
   B. the Society for the Prevention of Cruelty to Children
   C. a Family Court Judge
   D. a police officer

   3._____

4. Anthony, aged 8, has had many difficult experiences in his life. His father's whereabouts are unknown as he deserted when Anthony was two years old. His mother, whom he loved dearly, died three months ago. Since that time he has been living with his grandmother, who is old and ill, and cannot care for such an active little boy. Together the grandmother and you, the social service worker, have decided that placement in a foster home is essential for Anthony's well-being. You know he will resist any change in his living arrangements.

   4._____

According to acceptable case work practice, the BEST of the following methods for you to apply in this situation is to
- A. take the boy to his new home without telling him anything beforehand
- B. explain that it is necessary to move him and that he is going to a very nice place where he will be happy and have many things he does not have now
- C. tell him you are sorry if he feel bad about it, but grown-ups know best what is good for him and he will have to do what they say
- D. give the child a chance to get to know you before he is moved and to express his feelings in relation to the plan which is being made for him

5. Mrs. Mary Wooster, who has been caring for her 10-year-old orphaned niece, applies for aid to dependent children when her husband's income is reduced. If you are the social worker assigned to this case, you should tell Mrs. Wooster that her application
   - A. *cannot be accepted* for investigation because her niece must be removed from her home and placed out by the state
   - B. *can be accepted* for investigation because she falls within the group of relatives who are eligible to receive aid to dependent children
   - C. *cannot be accepted* for investigation because relatives other than parents are never granted help through aid to dependent children
   - D. *can be accepted* for investigation because her niece is her legal responsibility

5.____

6. A 15-year-old girl calls on you, the social service worker, to say that her mother is negligent and buys clothing for herself and treats her male friends to motion picture dates with her grant from aid to dependent children.
   According to the MOST generally accepted social case work principles, you should tell the girl that
   - A. the grant will be stopped immediately
   - B. she does not have to put up with that kind of environment and can arrange to leave her mother immediately
   - C. you will take this matter up with her mother and see her again at some future time
   - D. she should file a formal complaint against her mother

6.____

7. Assume that in making your first visit to the home of an applicant for aid to dependent children, you find the beds unmade, the dishes unwashed, and the furniture so dusty that you cannot find a clean place to sit down, although it is already 3:00 in the afternoon. The applicant has four small children.
   Under the circumstances described, you should inform the applicant that
   - A. she is ineligible for the grant because she does not give her children the proper physical environment
   - B. her application will be investigated and her eligibility determined
   - C. her application will be investigated but if her home is not cleaned up when you visit next week, her application will be rejected
   - D. if found eligible for aid to dependent children, she must take instruction in housekeeping from the social services center home economist

7.____

8. One of your clients finds it necessary to be away from home for two weeks and arranges with her mother to care for her children, for whom she receives an aid to dependent children grant, without notifying your department about this plan. You discover her absence, however, when making a periodic revisit to the client's apartment.
In view of these facts, it would be MOST advisable to
   A. stop the grant immediately inasmuch as you are unable to see the client at this time
   B. let the grant continue, as the temporary planned absence of the client does affect her eligibility
   C. tell the client's mother that a recipient of aid to dependent children may not leave her children even for a temporary period
   D. order the client's mother to wire her to return within two days or the grant will stop

9. When a relief recipient requests that the Department of Social Services take some action because her unemployed husband is indifferent to her and unconcerned about the welfare of their children, the social service worker should
   A. inform the husband that he will be cut out of the grant if he does not change his attitude
   B. advise the woman to separate and try to build a life apart from her husband
   C. tell the woman to appeal to the Domestic Relations Court to have her husband ordered to spend his evenings at home
   D. suggest that the woman discuss this matter with a private family agency

10. A woman appears at your social services center and asks for advice on what to do as she would like, if possible, to be able to remain at home with her three children, aged four, seven, and ten. She declares that her husband has been killed and she is unable to manage on her old age and survivors insurance. Assuming the facts to be true as stated, the social service worker should advise her
    A. to apply for aid to dependent children
    B. to try to find a job
    C. to apply for more money under old age and survivors insurance
    D. that there are no other public financial resources available in her case

11. A child born out of wedlock to a certain Miss Smith has been placed in a private foster home. Miss Smith is unable to pay anything toward the child's care and one day, in discussing the case with a worker at the Bureau of Child Welfare, she asks about visiting her little girl.
The MOST desirable reply for the social service worker to make in his situation would be that Miss Smith
    A. cannot visit the child because she would exert an adverse influence over her
    B. should not visit since she is not paying for the child's care

C. should not visit because it will be difficult for the child to explain to her friends that her mother is unmarried
D. has the same right as any other mother to visit her child

12. Eight-year-old Johnny, on whose account his mother is receiving aid to dependent children, is beginning to truant from school. Disturbed by the course of events, his mother appears at the social services center and informs you, her social service worker, that her efforts to stop Johnny's truancy have been unavailing.
You should tell Johnny's mother that
    A. the grant will be discontinued since Johnny's truancy is evidence of her failure as a parent
    B. she can be referred to a specialized agency in the community
    C. you will institute court action to remove Johnny from his home environment
    D. you will give her two months to straighten out the problem before taking further action

13. Suppose you, as social service worker, are considering institutional care for several different types of children for whom removal from present homes is indicated.
Of the following, the type LEAST suited for such care would be
    A. a child needing observation, study, and treatment for a severe crippling condition
    B. a 15-year-old boy who resents adult authority
    C. a family of six brothers and sisters who are devoted to each other
    D. a normal 3-year-old girl whose mother is dead and whose father is employed at night

14. It is generally agreed among psychologists that children need to have certain experiences in order to develop into healthy, well-integrated adults.
Of the following, it is MOST important to the development of the pre-adolescent child that he
    A. live in a good neighborhood
    B. have a room of his own
    C. have nice clothes
    D. have the feeling that he is loved and wanted by his parents

15. The only educative agency which can properly be thought of as really starting with a *clean slate* in developing a person's behavior is the
    A. family   B. play group
    C. church group   D. elementary school

16. The LEAST accurate of the following statements regarding intelligence is that
    A. a person's intelligence is not directly related to biological factors
    B. persons differ radically in the degree of intelligence which they have
    C. persons cannot learn beyond the limits of their native intelligence regardless of the amount and kind of effort they expend

D. ill health, isolation, and certain kinds of temperament may seriously limit the proportion of one's intelligence which he may actually be able to put to use

17. The GREATEST limitation on the general effectiveness of marriage courses in college curricula is
    A. there is no evidence to prove that such courses result in better matings and happier homes
    B. successful completion of such courses is no indication that the knowledge contained in the courses will be successfully applied by the students who have taken them
    C. there is no complete agreement as to whether the family, the church, or the school should be responsible for guiding marriage education
    D. most of the people who marry are ineligible to enroll in such courses

17.____

18. In the following instances, cooperative behavior which results from loyalty to the same objective is BEST exemplified by
    A. the citizens of a community forming a committee for the purpose of building a school
    B. employer and employee agreeing to a conference for the purpose of arriving at an equitable wage settlement
    C. people attending a championship tennis match held for charitable purposes
    D. during WWII, the citizens of a German community accepting employment in the local headquarters of the American Military Government

18.____

19. Among persons handicapped by blindness, the ones who may be expected to display a range of experience MOST comparable with that of normal persons are those who
    A. receive no special consideration from others
    B. are closely protected by their kinsmen and friends against the severe limitations imposed by their handicap
    C. are urged to greater attainments than would be expected of normal persons in order to compensate for their affliction
    D. are urged to understand their potentialities and limitations and are encouraged to make the most of their opportunities

19.____

20. From the social service point of view, the MOST desirable requisite for a potential social service worker to have at the outset is
    A. a desire to return full value for the taxpayer's dollar
    B. knowledge of eligibility requirements for relief
    C. understanding of the functions of the Department of Social Services
    D. a desire to help people meet their problems

20.____

21. From the case history on a client described as a delinquent individual, illiterate, shy, regarded by others with annoyance or condescension, who hardly ever engages in group activities and never goes to church, movies, or theater, the social service worker would be justified in forming the conclusion that

21.____

A. the social isolation is responsible for the delinquency
B. the delinquency is responsible for the social isolation
C. both the poverty and isolation are responsible for the delinquency
D. a single case is insufficient for the inference that social isolation is regularly associated with poverty and delinquency

22. If a repatriated citizen disembarks at the Port of New York in a destitute condition, his relief problem will be handled in the following manner: he will be cared for by the
    A. Department of Social Services and the Federal Security Agency will reimburse the city in full for the expense involved
    B. Department of Social Services and the State Board of Social Welfare will reimburse the city in full for the expense involved
    C. Department of Social Services and the State will reimburse the city for 80% of the expense involved
    D. Immigration and Naturalization Service without cost to the city

22.____

23. In the past, census figures sometimes showed that in the age groups from 55 up, the number of foreign-born in the United States was greater than would ordinarily be expected in our population.
The MOST reliable explanation for this condition was probably that
    A. foreigners outlived native Americans because only the hardier among them ventured to emigrate from their own countries
    B. there were comparatively few young people among the foreign-born because immigration had been materially reduced
    C. foreign-born children had a shorter life expectancy than native-born children of foreign or American parents
    D. the number of persons who emigrated from the United States to other countries at those times exceeded the number who entered this country in the same period

23.____

24. A small town without a hospital is located near a large city which boasts of its excellent medical facilities. These facilities are extended liberally to non-residents who come from adjacent centers which do not have hospitals of their own.
If it is shown statistically that the death rate of the small town is lower compared to that of the large city, the MOST logical inference for the alert social service worker to make is that
    A. small-town life is more healthful than living in a big city
    B. the statistical data have been improperly manipulated
    C. death rates should not be determined by political boundaries
    D. the deaths of non-residents have boosted the death rate of the large city

24.____

25. Of the types of mental breakdown listed below, the disorder that ordinarily occurs at the MOST advanced age is
    A. cerebral arteriosclerosis   B. neurasthenia
    C. dementia praecox   D. paresis

25.____

26. The parole movement for releasing prisoners before the expiration of their sentence has gained headway MOSTLY because of the assumption on the part of the taxpaying public that
    A. prison officials and parole officers can watch the paroled prisoner closely and help him adjust himself in the community at the same time
    B. recidivism is greater for persons serving their full sentence
    C. it sends the parolee out with an obligation rather than a score to settle
    D. total costs for prison administration are materially reduced when a large percentage of the prison population have their terms of incarceration reduced

27. Among the theories advanced in favor of providing unemployment relief, the one that should appear to the social service worker as MOST basic is that
    A. it is the responsible of the government to provide for those unable to provide for themselves
    B. people would work for very little and thereby bring down salaries if unemployment relief were not granted
    C. a wholesome economy can exist only when money is kept circulating
    D. every man has the right to a job

28. During a period of economic adjustment when unemployment is on the rise, the invention of a labor-saving device would, in the long run, be economically and culturally
    A. *unsound*, because it would stir up unrest among the organized labor groups
    B. *unsound*, because it would result in accelerating unemployment
    C. *sound*, because the rise of unemployment is a temporary phenomenon while the labor-saving device would add permanent values
    D. *sound*, because it would enable the user to produce more with the small working population still employed

29. Wage rates for women in the United States do not match those for men in many industries LARGELY because
    A. women tend to constitute a marginal supply of labor
    B. the social attitude has swung back to the position that *women's place is in the home*
    C. the organized labor movement has modified its traditional stand regarding *equal pay for equal work*
    D. women do not attain highly responsible positions in the business world as consistently as men

30. The inability of people to obtain employment during a time of economic depression is an example of the principle that
    A. anyone who really wants a job can get one if he tries hard enough
    B. the more capable people get jobs when jobs are scarce
    C. at certain times, employment is not available for many people irrespective of ability, character, or need
    D. full employment is a thing of the past

KEY (CORRECT ANSWERS)

1.	B	11.	D	21.	D
2.	D	12.	B	22.	A
3.	C	13.	D	23.	B
4.	D	14.	D	24.	D
5.	B	15.	A	25.	A
6.	C	16.	A	26.	A
7.	B	17.	D	27.	A
8.	B	18.	A	28.	C
9.	D	19.	D	29.	D
10.	A	20.	D	30.	C

TEST 3

DIRECTIONS: Each question or incomplete statement is followed by several suggested answers or completions. Select the one that BEST answers the question or completes the statement. *PRINT THE LETTER OF THE CORRECT ANSWER IN THE SPACE AT THE RIGHT.*

1. It is often held that cooperative activity is difficult to achieve because *individuals are basically selfish* and their alleged selfishness makes it difficult, if not impossible, to subordinate their individual wills to the collective enterprise.
 The CHIEF factor overlooked in such a conception of the matter is that
    A. there is no necessary discrepancy or conflict between selfishness and cooperation
    B. people do not seek to further their self-interest by competitive activity
    C. competition and cooperation are essentially alike
    D. most successful people are not selfish

2. Under the law it is always necessary to establish eligibility for public assistance. While the facts that must be established are clearly defined by law and by policy, the social service worker has a good deal of freedom in his choice of method.
 Of the methods given below for obtaining desired information from applicants for relief, the one considered the BEST interviewing method in social work practice, and therefore recommended to the social service worker is to
    A. work from an outline, asking the questions in the order in which they appear and requiring the applicant to give specific answers
    B. let the applicant tell what he has to say in his own way first, the social service worker then taking responsibility for asking questions on points not covered
    C. tell the applicant all the facts that it is necessary to have, then letting him give the information in any way he chooses
    D. verify all such facts as birth date, income, and past employment before seeing the applicant, then asking the applicant to fill in the remaining gaps when he is interviewed.

3. Suppose an applicant for relief objects to answering a question regarding his recent employment and asks, *What business is it of yours, young man?*
 As the social service worker conducting the interview, the MOST constructive course of action for you to take under the circumstances would be to
    A. tell the applicant you have no intention of prying into his personal affairs and go on to the next question
    B. refer the applicant to your supervisor
    C. rephrase the question so that only a *Yes* or *No* answer is required
    D. explain why the question is being asked

4. Continued contact with relief recipients is maintained by social service workers employed by the Department of Social Services MAINLY because
   A. changes in relief need to be made in accordance with financial changes in the family situation
   B. many people do not report changes in income promptly
   C. most people do not understand that reports of their earnings are required
   D. the department wishes to see that the relief given is properly used

5. Inasmuch as periodic visits to clients at home are required by the Department of Social Services, according to good case work practice, it is MOST desirable for the social service worker to
   A. visit without appointment as this gives him a chance to see the person and the house *as they really are* and forestalls changing things to create a different impression
   B. write giving an appointment time as this saves the social worker from visiting when people are not home and helps him to plan his work more efficiently
   C. write suggesting an appointment time so that the client may be prepared for the interview and the social worker uses his time economically
   D. advise all applicant during their first interview that they will be visited periodically but not be given definite appointments

6. Assuming that careful interpretation has been given but an applicant for public assistance refuses to accede to the necessary procedures to establish his eligibility for aid, the MOST preferable of the following courses of action for you to take would be to
   A. do nothing further
   B. grant temporary aid in the hope that the applicant will change his mind
   C. try to ascertain why the applicant feels as he does, but to respect his decision if he refuses to change his mind
   D. proceed to check on all the facts possible even though the applicant has not given his permission

7. The PRIMARY purpose in discussing with an applicant steps in determining his eligibility and the kind of verification of facts which the agency will need is to
   A. enable the applicant to understand the basis of eligibility and participate in determining it
   B. protect the position of the agency so that there will be no comeback if relief is not granted
   C. give the applicant an opportunity to modify any statement he may have made previously
   D. promote public relations for the agency, since the applicant will tell others how the agency is operating

8. The BEST of the following reasons for which a public social services agency should NOT insist on certain standards of cleanliness as a factor in eligibility to receive relief is that it is generally acknowledged that
   A. people have a right to decide how they will live, provided their mode of living does not hurt others

B. standards of cleanliness vary so much among people as to make one standard impracticable
C. a little dirt has never hurt anyone
D. it would take too much of the social service worker's time to maintain a constant check on this factor

9. When a client receives home relief, he
    A. gives up the right to manage his money in his own way
    B. is justified in assuming that he has proved his eligibility for relief and is free to use the money according to his best judgment
    C. is limited in spending the money only for expenditures itemized in the agency budget
    D. is obligated to keep an itemized list of his expenditures

9.____

10. The knowledge and understanding of situations and of people attained through social case work may well serve as a basis for sound action and for effective social welfare planning.
    The MOST logical assumption that the social service worker can draw from the above statement is that
    A. since social service planning is related to broad social issues and needs, it is unnecessary to consider the individual
    B. the individual is the only unit to be considered in the planning of effective social welfare programs
    C. all social planning should be directed primarily toward the individual and his needs
    D. knowledge of the individual attained through social case work can be effectively utilized in planning a broad social welfare program

10.____

11. Of the following, the LEAST valid reason for the maintenance of the case record in public social services administration is to
    A. furnish reference material for other workers
    B. improve the quality of service to the client
    C. show how the public funds are being expended
    D. reduce the complexities of the case to manageable proportions

11.____

12. A public social services agency will lean more on forms than a private agency in the same field of activity because
    A. forms simplify the recording responsibilities of newly appointed social service workers
    B. public social service records are of the family agency type
    C. the governmental framework requires a greater degree of standardization
    D. more interviews and visits are made in connection with public relief cases

12.____

13. In spite of the need which most of us have of finding rules and procedures to guide us, we must face the difficulty at the outset that there is no such thing as a model case.
    Of the following, the BEST justification for this statement is that
    A. records should be written to suit the case
    B. case recording should be patterned after the best models obtainable

13.____

4 (#3)

    C. rules cannot be applied to social case work because each case requires individual treatment
    D. the establishment of routine and procedures in social work is an ideal which cannot be realized

14. One of the following disclosures is made regarding an applicant for old-age assistance and he is accordingly disqualified to receive the grant requested. In the recommendation submitted by the social service worker, the applicant would be found ineligible because he   14.____
    A. is not a citizen
    B. has $1,000 in a bank account which he is saving for burial purposes
    C. has three married children and could probably live with one of them
    D. refuses to give information concerning a bank account of $50,000 which had been in his name until four months prior to his application

15. The homemaking center of the Department of Social Services furnishes the service of mother's aides to families for help in caring for their children because of the mother's temporary incapacity or absence. Mother's aides can assume responsibility for such household duties as feeding infants, preparing meals, cleaning the home, etc. They are mature, responsible women with previous homemaking experience who have passed a literacy test and have undergone a thorough physical examination.   15.____
According to current thinking in the field, for the social service worker assigned in any case where a mother's aide is furnished, to use the mother's aide as a source of obtaining confidential information for the Department of Social Services would be
    A. *advisable*; as a result of contact with the family, the mother's aide will have observed many details concerning their daily activities
    B. *inadvisable*; while the mother's aide will have observed many details concerning the daily activities of the family, she has not been trained to interpret these observations
    C. *advisable*; the mother's aide has been thoroughly examined as to her ability to perform her duties in the household
    D. *inadvisable*; the mother's aide has a primary obligation to the family rather than to the Department of Social Services

16. When a family asks the help of the social service worker because they are consistently exceeding their food and clothing allowance, the social service worker should   16.____
    A. use the services of the home economist for consultation on the management problem which has developed
    B. order the family to live within their budget allowance
    C. ignore the situation as it is the family's responsibility to make ends meet
    D. recommend small increases in the food and clothing allowance for this family

17. When a landlord complains to the social service worker that a certain relief recipient has consistently neglected to pay his rent, present case work practice would indicate to the social service worker that he should FIRST
    A. arrange to discontinue relief payments until he can verify the reasons for the non-payment of rent
    B. tell the client to pay his rent within a certain period of time if he does not want his relief discontinued
    C. tell the client about the landlord's complaint and inform him the Department of Social Services assumes that rent is an obligation the client is expected to settle directly with his landlord
    D. arrange for the landlord to collect his rent at the social services center in the future

Questions 18-23.

DIRECTIONS: Questions 18 through 23, inclusive, deal with social service allowances of various kinds. Assuming that in the Department of Social Services the allowance schedules shown below are among those included in estimating the needs of relief recipients, use the figures given to determine your answers. All figure are quoted on a monthly basis.

Item	Allowance
Rent	As paid by client
Utilities	$12 per person
Person Incidentals	$7 per person

	Adult	Child 13-18	Child Under 13
Food	$360	$350	$300
Clothing	90	84	79

18. The Anderson family consisting of father, mother, and four children aged 4, 10, 15, and 17, is eligible for home relief. The rent is $800 a month. Relief granted on the basis of the above items is given semi-monthly.
    According to the above schedule, the proper semi-monthly grant for this family would be
    A. $1,076   B. $1,427   C. $1,717   D. $3,134

19. Assuming that all the expenditures except rent were reimbursed under the State Welfare Law to the same extent that reimbursements for home relief are now being made to the city, the annual cost to the city for all the items included in the public assistance budget of the Anderson family would be APPROXIMATELY
    A. $8,400   B. $16,000   C. $24,000   D. $28,000

20. Mrs. Peet is 67 years old and applies for old-age assistance. She lives with her widowed niece who has a family of three children. The rent of the apartment is $560 a month. The niece has agreed to pay for the utilities of the whole group and also to give Mrs. Peet some money for personal incidentals, provided that Mrs. Peet can pay one-fifth of the rent. On medical advice, a special diet allowance of $77.20 a month is authorized for Mrs. Peet in addition to the regular food allowance.
The proper monthly grant for Mrs. Peet would be
A. $498.80   B. $560.75   C. $639.20   D. $1,006.50

21. Mrs. Scalise applies for relief for herself and her two children aged two and four. Her rent costs $650 a month. She is separated from her husband, who contributes $180 a week by court order. It has also been verified that Mrs. Scalise earns $112 a week doing piece-work at home.
Assuming that for budget computation purposes the Department of Social Services considers 4.3 weeks as equivalent to one month, the monthly grant in this case would be
A. $538.10   B. $659.40   C. $938.00   D. $1,012.20

22. A 36-year-old sightless widower applies for aid to the blind. His rent and utilities are met by relatives with whom he lives. In aid to blind cases, $92 per month is allowed for expenses incident to blindness as a substitute for the personal incidentals item in the above schedule.
Under these circumstances, the proper monthly grant would be
A. $342.50   B. $537.00   C. $646.50   D. $1,057.50

23. John Burke is 52 years old and needs supplementary home relief. He pays $370 a month for his room and he earn $420 a month doing odd jobs. Basing your computations on these facts and on the above schedule, you can determine that the proper semi-monthly grant for Mr. Burke would be
A. $508.50   B. $369.60   C. $209.50   D. $163.00

24. In attempting to discover whether an applicant for aid to dependent children has had any previous experience as a relief recipient through other social service agencies in the community, the social service worker should
A. check the application for such aid with the social service exchange
B. send the fingerprints of the applicant to the Police Department
C. consult the latest records of the Department of Social Services
D. ask the applicant to submit a notarized statement to the effect that such aid has not been received from any other source

25. Mr. Ritter asks the Department of Social Services to place his son, aged five, in a foster home. In a subsequent interview, Mr. Ritter refuses to divulge what sources of income are at his disposal.
As the social service worker trying to obtain this information, you should explain to Mr. Ritter that
A. you want to know whether he is seeking placement for his son because he does not want to provide for him financially

B. part of placement procedure involves determining the extent of financial responsibility parents can continue to assume
C. if he makes no payment his parental rights will be affected
D. the frequency of his visits will depend on the amount of support he continues to furnish

26. A woman applying for supplementation of her earnings explains that she earns $300 weekly but that the doctor has advised her to work only four days a week in order to safeguard her health. Under the reduced schedule, her earnings would drop to $200 a week and she would be unable to continue supporting her 62-year-old mother.
Assuming that this information has been duly verified, the woman's request for supplementary relief should be
    A. *granted*, because she supports her old mother
    B. *not granted*, because she can still manage to work a full week
    C. *granted*, because the reduction of work is necessary to preserve her health
    D. *not granted*, because her mother can get old-age assistance

27. Suppose a client whom you are investigating has borrowed $250 in order to purchase an evening gown for one of her children who is being graduated from high school. She is planning to repay the loan at the rate of $10 a week, and presents verification of this transaction as well as of the purchase.
As a social service worker, you would be complying with the BEST case work principles by
    A. telling the client her grant will be reduced in view of her ability to manage on $10 less each week
    B. telling the clerk that she must never do this again
    C. explaining to the client how her action will make it more difficult for the family to get along on their limited grant
    D. suggesting that she return the dress and repay the borrowed money in this way

28. Mrs. Rose complains to the social service worker about the inadequacy of her relief allowance although she is being granted the maximum amount for a person in her situation. It is acknowledged by the Department of Social Services that the amount of the grant is not based on current prices.
Under these circumstances, the MOST considerate reply the social service worker can make to this complainant is that
    A. the grant is based on a scientific calculation of needs for subsistence and is only a small percentage short of what is actually needed
    B. the social service worker knows it is difficult to manage since the cost of living was steadily rising, but that the amount granted was all the Department of Social Services schedule allows at the present time
    C. Mrs. Rose would be worse off if there were no public assistance
    D. many people in other countries do not have even the small grant allowed Mrs. Rose

29. Miss Lowe applies for assistance and is able to account for her work history and her financial expenditures with the exception of three months in 2020.
As acting intake interviewer, it would be your responsibility to inform her that
   A. she will remain ineligible until she accounts for her complete work history
   B. her application can be accepted, but that certain verification will have to be made as to her statements regarding lack of resources
   C. she is obviously hiding pertinent information and that her application cannot therefore be considered
   D. she obviously had some sources in 2020 and that she should use this source again

30. Knowing that a client needs a period of rest and that another agency can arrange this, it would be the responsibility of a social service worker to
   A. notify the client of this resource and suggest that he apply there if he wishes to
   B. try to make all the arrangements for the client, telling the other agency he knows all about the client's situation and can apply for him
   C. tell the client that unless he applies to the other agency, he will do so for him
   D. tell the client he seems insufficiently interested in getting well enough to work and the Department of Social Services may discontinue his assistance

31. An irate citizen comes into the Social Services office protesting that William Case, a relief recipient, made no effort to shop most economically and was therefore wasting public funds which he, a taxpayer, in part contributed. The complainant wants to know why Mr. Case was given cash instead of a food voucher.
The social service worker should tell this citizen that the Department of Social Services will not transfer Mr. Case to voucher relief because cash relief
   A. is easier to administer
   B. enables the investigator to know how responsible a person is by the way he spends his money
   C. enables people to maintain their usual way of living
   D. keeps money in circulation

32. Assume that a certain Mr. Sears applied for relief three weeks ago. As he has not yet received an assistance, he comes to see the social service worker to find out why he is being neglected. A checkup of Mr. Sears' status reveals that his application has been inactive pending receipt of a reply from a former employer. When informed of this contingency, Mr. Sears offers to expedite matters by getting in touch with the employer himself.
The BEST way for the social service worker to handle this case would be to tell Mr. Sears that
   A. the determination of his eligibility is the responsibility of the social service worker alone
   B. it would help if he could hurry the reply
   C. if he discusses this with the employer, the information will be invalidated
   D. he should just go home and wait

33. When he applies for public relief, a man gives a complete and straightforward account of his past employment and earnings, of the inability of his relatives to help, and of his attempts to find work. The way the family has managed in the past indicates excellent planning ability in the use of money and making limited resources go a long way. He says he exhausted all resources before applying, and gives a detailed account. The family lived on less than a relief allowance while receiving unemployment compensation. They have exhausted their credit at the grocery store. The landlord is threatening eviction because of rent arrears of two months. He explains he went through all this because it is so painful for him to apply for relief. The man is obviously honest and reliable. Under these circumstances, a conscientious social service worker would find that
    A. it is unnecessary to verify the foregoing information in order to establish eligibility
    B. it is necessary to verify the facts given above in order to establish eligibility
    C. the interviewer should be free to decide whether any verifications are needed
    D. eligibility considerations should be waived and an immediate grant made in order to help the man feel better

34. Mr. Russell complains to his social service worker that he is too feeble to cook his own food and needs more money in order to eat in restaurants.
    If investigation of the request proves that Mr. Russell's condition is as indicated, the social service worker should
    A. explain why no provision can be made for this additional expense
    B. suggest that Mr. Russell get a neighbor to help with the cooking
    C. recommend that the allowance be increased
    D. explain that relief recipients should not eat in restaurants

35. When applying for unemployment relief, a prospective client states that he can get a job immediately at $300 a week but that he has hesitated to accept such employment because he feels his income would be inadequate to support his family which, besides himself, includes his wife and two children. The applicant also states that he has enrolled in a training program which, if he can pursue to a satisfactory conclusion two weeks hence, will enable him to accept a job paying $500 weekly.
    If you were the social service worker in this case, the MOST constructive of the following courses of action for you to take would be to
    A. recommend that relief be given immediately
    B. recommend that relief not be given because the applicant has a $300 job available to him
    C. tell the applicant he must take the $300 job and then give him supplementation on account of his inadequate earnings
    D. recommend relief if the information is verified

KEY (CORRECT ANSWERS)

1.	A	11.	D	21.	B	31.	C
2.	B	12.	C	22.	B	32.	B
3.	D	13.	A	23.	C	33.	B
4.	A	14.	D	24.	A	34.	C
5.	C	15.	B	25.	B	35.	D
6.	C	16.	A	26.	C		
7.	A	17.	C	27.	C		
8.	A	18.	C	28.	B		
9.	B	19.	B	29.	B		
10.	D	20.	C	30.	A		

EXAMINATION SECTION
TEST 1

DIRECTIONS: Each question or incomplete statement is followed by several suggested answers or completions. Select the one that BEST answers the question or completes the statement. *PRINT THE LETTER OF THE CORRECT ANSWER IN THE SPACE AT THE RIGHT.*

1. The PRIMARY function of the Department of Social Services is to
   A. refer needy persons to legally responsible relatives for support
   B. enable needy persons to become self-supporting
   C. refer ineligible persons to private agencies
   D. grant aid to needy eligible persons
   E. administer public assistance programs in which the federal and state governments do not participate

2. A public assistance program objective should be designed to
   A. provide for eligible persons in accordance with their individual requirements and with consideration of the circumstances in which they live
   B. provide for eligible persons at a standard of living equal to that enjoyed while they were self-supporting
   C. make sure that assistance payments from public funds are not too liberal
   D. guard against providing a better living for persons receiving aid than is enjoyed by the most frugal independent families
   E. eliminate the need for private welfare agencies

3. It is often stated that it would be better to abolish the need for relief rather than to extend the existing public assistance programs.
   This statement suggests that
   A. existing legislation makes it too easy for people to apply for and receive assistance
   B. public assistance should be limited to institutional care for rehabilitative purposes
   C. the support of needy persons should be the responsibility of their own families and relatives rather than that of the government
   D. the existing criteria used to determine *need* for public assistance are too liberal and should be modified to include a *work* test
   E. attempts should be made to eradicate those forces in our social organization which cause poverty

4. The one of the following types of public assistance which is frequently described as a *special privilege* is
   A. veteran assistance
   B. emergency assistance
   C. aid to dependent children
   D. old-age assistance
   E. vocational rehabilitation of the handicapped

25

5. The principle of *settlement* holds that each community is responsible for the care of its own members and that communities should not bear the costs of care for needy non-residents.
   This was an intrinsic principle of the
   A. English Poor Laws
   B. Home Rule Amendment
   C. Single Tax Proposal
   D. National Bankruptcy Regulations
   E. Proportional Representation Act

5.____

6. The FIRST form of state social security legislation developed in the United States was
   A. health insurance
   B. unemployment compensation
   C. workmen's compensation
   D. old-age insurance
   E. old-age assistance

6.____

7. The plan for establishing a federal department with Cabinet status to be known as the Department of Health, Education, and Welfare, was
   A. vetoed by the President after having been passed by Congress
   B. disapproved by the Senate after having been passed by the House of Representatives
   C. rejected by both the Senate and the House of Representatives
   D. enacted into legislation during a past session of Congress
   E. determined to be unconstitutional

7.____

8. Census Bureau reports show certain definite social trends in our population. One of these trends which was a major contributing factor in the establishment of the federal old-age insurance system was the
   A. increased rate of immigration to the United States
   B. rate at which the number of Americans living to 65 years of age and beyond is increasing
   C. increasing amounts spent for categorical relief in the country as a whole
   D. decreasing number of legally responsible relatives who have been unable to assist the aged since the Depression of 1929
   E. number of states which have failed to meet their obligations in the care of the aged

8.____

9. The Federal Housing Administration is the agency which
   A. insures mortgages made by lending institutions for new construction or remodeling of old construction
   B. provides federal aid for state and local governments for slum clearance and housing for very low income families
   C. subsidizes the building industry through direct grants
   D. provides for the construction of low-cost housing projects owned and operated by the federal government
   E. combines city planning with government subsidies for large-scale housing

9.____

10. Reports show that more men than women are physically handicapped MAINLY because
    A. women are instinctively more cautious than men
    B. men are more likely to have congenital deformities
    C. women tend to see surgical remedies because of greater concern over personal appearance
    D. men have lower ability to recover from injury
    E. men are more likely to be exposed to hazardous conditions

11. Of the following, the explanation married women give MOST frequently for seeking employment outside the home is that they wish to
    A. escape the drudgeries of home life
    B. develop secondary employment skills
    C. maintain an emotionally satisfying career
    D. provide the main support for the family
    E. supplement the family income

12. Of the following home conditions, the one MOST likely to cause emotional disturbances in children is
    A. increased birthrate following the war
    B. disrupted family relationships
    C. lower family income than that of neighbors
    D. higher family income than that of neighbors
    E. overcrowded living conditions

13. Casual unemployment, as distinguished from other types of unemployment, is traceable MOST readily to
    A. a decrease in the demand for labor as a result of scientific progress
    B. more or less haphazard changes in the demand for labor in certain industries
    C. periodic changes in the demand for labor in certain industries
    D. disturbances and disruptions in industry resulting from international trade barriers
    E. increased mobility of the population

14. Labor legislation, although primarily intended for the benefit of the employee, may aid the employer by
    A. increasing his control over the immediate labor market
    B. prohibiting government interference with operating policies
    C. protecting him, through equalization of labor costs, from being undercut by other employers
    D. transferring to the general taxpayer the principal costs of industrial hazards of accident and unemployment
    E. increasing the pensions of civil service employees

15. When employment and unemployment figures both decline, the MOST probable conclusion is that
    A. the population has reached a condition of equilibrium
    B. seasonal employment has ended

C. the labor force has decreased
D. payments for unemployment insurance have been increased
E. industrial progress has reduced working hours

16. In evaluating the adequacy of an individual's income, a social service worker should place primary emphasis on
    A. its value in relation to the average income
    B. the source of the income
    C. its relation to the earning capacity of the individual
    D. its purchasing power
    E. the purposes for which it is spent

16._____

17. An individual with an I.Q. of 100 may be said to have demonstrated _____ intelligence.
    A. superior
    B. absolute
    C. substandard
    D. approximately average
    E. high average

17._____

18. While state legislatures differ in many respects, all of them are MOST NEARLY alike in
    A. provisions for retirement of members
    B. rate of pay
    C. length of legislative sessions
    D. method of selection of their members
    E. length of term of office

18._____

19. If a state passed a law in a field under Congressional jurisdiction and if Congress subsequently passed contrary legislation, the state provision would be
    A. regarded as never having existed
    B. valid until the next session of the state legislature which would be obliged to repeal it
    C. superseded by the federal statute
    D. ratified by Congress
    E. still operative in the state involved

19._____

20. Power to pardon offenses committed against the people of the United States is vested in the
    A. Supreme Court of the United States
    B. United States District Courts
    C. Federal Bureau of Investigation
    D. United States Parole Board
    E. President of the United States

20._____

21. As distinguished from formal social control of an individual's behavior, an example of informal social control is that exerted by
    A. public opinion
    B. religious doctrine
    C. educational institutions
    D. statutes
    E. public health measures

21._____

22. The PRINCIPAL function of the jury in a jury trial is to decide questions of 22.____
    A. equity   B. fact   C. injunction
    D. contract   D. law

23. Of the following rights of an individual, the one which usually depends on 23.____
    citizenship as distinguished from those given anyone living under the laws of
    the United States is the right to
    A. receive public assistance
    B. hold an elective office
    C. petition the government for redress of grievances
    D. receive equal protection of the laws
    E. be accorded a trial by jury

24. The name of Thomas Malthus is MOST closely associated with a work on 24.____
    A. population   B. political justice   C. capitalism
    D. social contract E. wealth of nations

25. A chronic functional disease characterized by fits or attacks in which there 25.____
    is a loss of consciousness with a succession of convulsions is called
    A. epilepsy   B. dipsomania   C. catalepsy
    D. Hodgkin's disease E. paresis

KEY (CORRECT ANSWERS)

1.	D	11.	E
2.	A	12.	B
3.	E	13.	B
4.	A	14.	C
5.	A	15.	C
6.	C	16.	D
7.	D	17.	D
8.	B	18.	D
9.	A	19.	C
10.	E	20.	E

21.	A
22.	B
23.	B
24.	A
25.	A

TEST 2

DIRECTIONS: Each question or incomplete statement is followed by several suggested answers or completions. Select the one that BEST answers the question or completes the statement. *PRINT THE LETTER OF THE CORRECT ANSWER IN THE SPACE AT THE RIGHT.*

Questions 1-10.

DIRECTIONS: Questions 1 through 10, inclusive, are based on the following table, which gives a partial summary of certain groups of cases in the social services center of a public assistance agency.

SOCIAL SERVICES CENTER CASELOAD SUMMARY, JUNE-SEPTEMBER

	June	July	August	September
Total Cases Under Care at End of Month	13,790	11,445	13,191	12,209
Home relief	4,739	2,512	6,055	5,118
Old-age assistance	5,337	b	5,440	2,265
Aid to dependent children	3,487	1,621	1,520	4,594
Aid to the Blind	227	251	176	232
Net Change During Month	-344	c	1,746	-982
Applications Made During Month	1,542	789	3,153	1,791
Total Cases Accepted during Month	534	534	2,879	982
Home relief	278	213	342	338
Old-age assistance	43	161	1,409	f
Aid to dependent children	195	153	1,115	307
Aid to the blind	18	7	13	14
Total Cases Closed During Month	878	d	1,133	1,964
To private employment	326	1,197	460	870
To unemployment insurance	96	421	126	205
Reclassified	176	326	178	399
All other reasons	280	935	e	490
Total Cases Carried Over to Next Month	a	11,445	13,191	12,209

1. The number which should be placed in the blank indicated by *a* is
   A. 12,912   B. 13,446   C. 13,790
   D. 14,134   E. None of the above

   1.____

2. The number which should be placed in the blank indicated by *b* is
   A. 6,385   B. 7,601   C. 8,933
   D. 7,061   E. None of the above

   2.____

3. The number which should be placed in the blank indicated by *c* is
   A. -2,345   B. -344   C. 344
   D. 3,413   E. None of the above

   3.____

2 (#2)

4. The number which should be placed in the blank indicated by *d* is
   A. 2,789 B. 2,345 C. 7,601
   D. 3,879 E. None of the above

5. Of the total number of cases closed during the month of August, the percentage closed for reasons other than reclassification or receipt of unemployment insurance is APPROXIMATELY
   A. 13.8% B. 73.17% C. 26.83% D. 40.60% E. 24.63%

6. In comparing June and July, the figures indicate that with respect to the total cases under care at the end of each month,
   A. the percentage of total cases accepted during the month was lower in June
   B. the percentage of total cases accepted during the month was higher in June
   C. the percentage of total cases accepted during both months was the same
   D. there were more cases under care at the end of July
   E. there is insufficient data for comparison of the total cases under care at the end of each month

7. The total number of cases accepted during the entire period in the category in which most cases were accepted was
   A. 1,409 B. 1,936 C. 1,770 D. 4,929 E. 20,103

8. In comparing July and September, the figures indicate that
   A. more cases were closed in September because of private employment
   B. the total number of cases accepted during the month consisted of a greater proportion of home relief cases in September
   C. in one of these months, there were more total cases under care at the end of the month than at the beginning of the month
   D. aid to dependent children cases at the beginning of September numbered almost three times as many as at the beginning of July
   E. none of the above is correct

9. The total number of applications made during the four-month period was
   A. more than four times the number of cases closed because of private employment during the same period
   B. less than the combined totals of aid to dependent children cases under care in June and July
   C. 4,376 more than the total number of cases accepted during August
   D. 23 times as large as the number of cases reclassified in July
   E. 5,916 less than the total number of cases carried over to September

10. The ratio of old-age assistance cases accepted in August to the total number of such cases under care at the end of that month is expressed with the GREATEST degree of accuracy by the figures
    A. 1:4 B. 1:25 C. 4:1 D. 7:128 E. 10:39

11. The term *mores* refers to
    A. English meadows   B. bribery   C. Moorish worship
    D. telegraphic code   E. social customs

12. *Disparity* refers MOST directly to
    A. difference   B. argument   C. low wages
    D. separation   E. injustice

13. The technical term used to express the ratio between mental and chronological age is called the
    A. mentality rating   B. culture level index
    C. psychometric standard   D. achievement index
    E. intelligence quotient

14. In social services work, the disorganizing factors in a personal or familial situation which prevent or hinder rehabilitation are called
    A. median deviations   B. transference situations
    C. rank correlations   D. liabilities
    E. collective representations

15. The period in the life of man when mental abilities begin to deteriorate is known as
    A. puberty   B. adolescence   C. gerontology
    D. senility   E. antiquity

Questions 16-25.

DIRECTIONS: Questions 16 through 25, inclusive, contain two blank spaces each. You are to select the words which will fill the blanks so that the sentence will be true and sensible. For the *first* blank in each question, select a word or phrase preceded by letter A, B, C, D, or E. For the *second* blank in the question, select a word or phrase preceded by letter V, W, X, Y, or Z. Use the two letters you have selected as your answer and print both these letters in the correspondingly numbered space at the right.

16. _____ is to public assistance as citizenship is to _____.
    A. need   B. school attendance   C. worthiness
    D. child   E. welfare center
    V. passport   W. alien   X. immigration
    Y. excise tax   Z. indictment

17. _____ is to home relief as public institutional care is to _____.
    A. compensation   B. supplementation
    C. direct relief   D. survivor's insurance
    E. fiscal period
    V. removal of custody W. adoption
    X. indoor relief   Y. day care
    Z. voucher assistance

18. _____ is to face sheet as income is to _____. 18._____
    A. client   B. cash relief
    C. relief standard   D. case record
    E. emergency assistance
    V. wages   W. home
    X. debts   Y. taxes
    Z. bonus

19. _____ is to demography as man is to _____. 19._____
    A. politics   B. racial relations   C. stigmata
    D. social statistics E. democracy
    V. population   W. geography   X. woman
    Y. marriage   Z. anthropology

20. _____ is to tuberculosis as Terman is to _____. 20._____
    A. Wasserman   B. Mantoux   C. Schick
    D. Ascheim-Zondek   E. Snellen
    V. litmus test   W. means test   X. lie detector test
    Y. intelligence test Z. CAVD test

21. _____ is to dementia as feeblemindedness is to _____. 21._____
    A. anger   B. luxation   C. insanity
    D. diagnosis   E. psychiatry
    V. myopia   W. amentia   X. tibia
    Y. criminal   Z. childhood

22. Frustration is to _____ as _____ is to relaxation. 22._____
    A. satisfaction   B. goal   C. need
    D. desire   E. motive
    V. tension   W. behavior   X. adjustment
    Y. readjustment   Z. reaction

23. _____ is to embezzlement as parole is to _____. 23._____
    A. intent   B. larceny   C. desertion
    D. guilt   E. conviction
    V. bail   W. plea   X. probation
    Y. innocence   Z. reformatory

24. Abandonment is to _____ as coercion is to _____. 24._____
    A. abduction   B. discovery   C. guardian
    D. adultery   E. desertion
    V. desertion   W. impotence   X. crime
    Y. coition   Z. constraint

25. _____ is to homicide as felony is to _____. 25._____
    A. courthouse   B. mayhem   C. negligence
    D. witness   E. manslaughter
    V. judge   W. crime   X. autopsy
    Y. civil suit   Z. prosecutor

KEY (CORRECT ANSWERS)

1. C
2. D
3. A
4. E
5. B

6. A
7. B
8. E
9. E
10. E

11. E
12. A
13. E
14. D
15. D

16. AV
17. CX
18. DV
19. DZ
20. BY

21. CW
22. AV
23. BX
24. EZ
25. EW

TEST 3

DIRECTIONS: Each question or incomplete statement is followed by several suggested answers or completions. Select the one that BEST answers the question or completes the statement. *PRINT THE LETTER OF THE CORRECT ANSWER IN THE SPACE AT THE RIGHT.*

Questions 1-3.

DIRECTIONS: Questions 1 through 3, inclusive, are to be answered on the basis of the following passage.

Aid to dependent children shall be given to a parent or other relative as herein specified for the benefit of a child or children under sixteen years of age or of a minor or minors between sixteen and eighteen years of age if in the judgment of the administrative agency: (1) the granting of an allowance will be in the interest of such child or minor, and (2) the parent or other relative is a fit person to bring up such child or minor so that his physical, mental, and moral well-being will be safeguarded, and (3) aid is necessary to enable such parent or other relative to do so, and (4) such child or minor is a resident of the state on the date of application for aid, and (5) such minor between sixteen and eighteen years of age is regularly attending school in accordance with the regulations of the department. An allowance may be granted for the aid of such child or minor who has been deprived or parental support or care by reason of the death, continued absence from the home, or physical or mental incapacity of a parent, and who is living with his father, mother, grandfather, grandmother, brother, sister, stepfather, stepmother, stepbrother, stepsister, uncle or aunt. In making such allowances, consideration shall be given to the ability of the relative making application and of any other relatives to support and care for or to contribute to the support and care of such child or minor. In making all such allowances, it shall be made certain that the religious faith of the child or minor shall be preserved and protected.

1. The preceding passage is concerned PRIMARILY with
   A. the financial ability of persons applying for public assistance
   B. compliance on the part of applicants with the *settlement* provisions of the law
   C. the fitness of parents or other relatives to bring up physically, mentally, or morally delinquent children between the ages of sixteen and eighteen
   D. eligibility for aid to dependent children
   E. the religious faith of children or minors coming within the provisions of this law

2. On the basis of the preceding passage, the MOST accurate of the following statements is:
   A. Mary Doe, mother of John, age 18, is entitled to aid for her son if he is attending school regularly
   B. Evelyn Stowe, mother of Eleanor, age 13, is not entitled to aid for Eleanor if she uses her home for immoral purposes
   C. Ann Roe, cousin of Helen, age 14, is entitled to aid for Helen if the latter is living with her
   D. Peter Moe, uncle of Henry, age 15, is not entitled to aid for Henry if the latter is living with him

1.____

2.____

E. Harriet Hoe, mother of Paul, age 7, is not entitled to aid for him if she has been divorced from her husband

3. The above passage is PROBABLY an excerpt of the
   A. Administrative Code
   B. Social Welfare Law
   C. Federal Security Act
   D. City Charter
   E. Colonial Laws of the state

   3._____

4. Recent amendment of the Social Security Act has produced major changes in the administration of public assistance.
   The one of the following which is NOT included among these changes is the
   A. availability of federal funds in matching payments for home relief to veterans who are employable but unemployed
   B. establishment of federal grants-in-aid for a category of assistance to be known as aid to the permanently and totally disabled
   C. extension of the four categories of assistance to Puerto Rico and the Virgin Islands
   D. sharing by the federal government of costs of assistance to needy aged and blind persons in public medical institutions
   E. availability of federal funds within present federal maxima in matching indirect payments for medical care in old-age assistance, aid to the blind, and aid to dependent children

   4._____

5. The length of residence required to make a person eligible for the various forms of public assistance available in the United States
   A. is the same in all states but is different among public assistance programs in a given state
   B. is the same in all states and among different public assistance programs in a given state
   C. is the same in all states for different categories
   D. varies among states and among different public assistance programs in a given state
   E. varies only in the local agencies of a given state

   5._____

6. The Social Welfare Law requires that whenever an applicant for aid to dependent children resides in a place where there is a central index or a social service exchange, the public welfare official shall register the case with such index or exchange.
   This requirement is for the purpose of
   A. preventing duplication and coordinating the work of public and private agencies
   B. establishing prior claims on the amounts of assistance furnished when repayments are made
   C. having the social service exchange determine which agency should handle the case
   D. providing statistical data regarding the number of persons receiving grants for aid to dependent children
   E. making sure that opportunities for private employment are available to persons receiving assistance

   6._____

7. A person who knowingly brings a needy person from another state into the state for the purpose of making him a public charge, is guilty of
    A. violation of the Displaced Persons Act
    B. violation of the Mann Act
    C. a felony
    D. a misdemeanor
    E. no offense

    7._____

8. Among the following needy persons, the one NOT eligible to receive veteran assistance is the
    A. husband of a veteran, if living with the veteran
    B. minor grandchild of a veteran, if living with the veteran
    C. incapacitated child of a deceased veteran
    D. stepmother of stepfather of a veteran, if living with the veteran
    E. non-veteran brother or sister of a veteran, if living with the veteran

    8._____

9. The term *state residence*, as defined in the Social Welfare Law, means continuous residence within the state for a period of AT LEAST
    A. one year   B. two years   C. six months
    D. one month   E. one day

    9._____

10. In order to be eligible for old-age assistance in this state, applicants must have resided continuously in the state prior to the date of application for
    A. three months   B. six months   C. one year
    D. five years   E. no specific period

    10._____

11. Under the Social Security Act, public assistance payments do NOT provide for
    A. old-age assistance
    B. care of children in foster homes
    C. aid to the blind
    D. aid to dependent children
    E. aid to the permanently and totally disabled

    11._____

12. The Social Welfare Law provides that certain relatives of a recipient of public assistance or care, or of a person liable to become in need thereof, be responsible for the support of such person if they are of sufficient ability. The one of the following who is NOT a legally responsible relative is a(n)
    A. mother
    B. child
    C. grandparent
    D. uncle
    E. step-parent, for a minor stepchild

    12._____

13. Of the following, the distinguishing characteristics of a *dependent child* as defined in the Social Welfare Law, refer to a child who is
    A. in the custody of, or wholly or partly maintained by an authorized organization of charitable, eleemosynary, correctional, or reformatory character

    13._____

B. in such condition of want or suffering or who under improper guardianship as to injure or endanger the morals of himself or others
C. between 16 and 18 years of age and solely dependent upon his parents for support and maintenance
D. under 16 years of age and deserted or abandoned by parents or other persons lawfully charged with his care
E. incorrigible or ungovernable and beyond the control of his parents or guardian

14. Recent adoption laws tend to place increased emphasis upon
    A. informal signing of adoption papers
    B. lowered residence requirements for adoption
    C. establishment of the child's inheritance rights
    D. social investigation of the home before adoption
    E. increased boarding rates paid to adoptive parents

15. Any person or organization soliciting donations in public places is required to have a license issued by the
    A. Police Department
    B. Department of Sanitation
    C. Division of Labor Relations
    D. Department of Social Services
    E. Department of Licenses

16. A person who, though himself, in good health, harbors disease germs which may be passed on to others, is called a(n)
    A. instigator
    B. carrier
    C. incubator
    D. inoculator
    E. malingerer

17. Diseases most commonly caused by certain working environments or conditions are known as _____ diseases.
    A. infectious
    B. contagious
    C. occupational
    D. hereditary
    E. compensatory

18. The process of destroying micro-organisms which cause disease or infection is called
    A. contamination
    B. immunization
    C. inoculation
    D. sterilization
    E. infestation

19. Proper utilization of the term *carious* would involve reference to
    A. teeth
    B. curiosity
    C. shipment of food packages to needy persons in Europe
    D. hazardous or precarious situations
    E. lack of reasonable precautions

20. The chemical agent which has been used extensively to prevent the spread of typhus infection is
    A. cortisone
    B. D.D.T.
    C. penicillin
    D. ephedrine
    E. sulfanilamide

21. The medical term for *hardening of the arteries* is 21.____
    A. carcinoma B. arthritis C. thrombosis
    D. arteriosclerosis E. phlebitis

22. A set of symptoms which occur together is called a 22.____
    A. sympathin B. syncope C. syndrome
    D. synecdoche E. syllogism

23. If the characteristics of a person were being studied by competent observers, 23.____
    it would be expected that their observations would differ MOST markedly with
    respect to their evaluation of the person's
    A. intelligence B. nutritional characteristics
    C. temperamental characteristics D. weight
    E. height

24. If there are evidences of dietary deficiency in families where cereals make up 24.____
    a major portion of the diet, the MOST likely reason for this deficiency is that
    A. cereals cause absorption of excessive quantities of water
    B. persons who concentrate their diet on cereals do not chew their food
       properly
    C. carbohydrates are deleterious
    D. other essential food elements are omitted
    E. children eat cereals too rapidly

25. Although malnutrition is generally associated with poverty, dietary studies of 25.____
    population groups in the United States reveal that
    A. malnutrition is most often due to a deficiency of nutrients found chiefly in
       high-cost foods
    B. there has been overemphasis of the causal relationship between poverty
       and malnutrition
    C. malnutrition is found among people with sufficient money to be well fed
    D. a majority of the population in all income groups is undernourished
    E. malnutrition is not a factor in the incidence of rickets

KEY (CORRECT ANSWERS)

1.	D		11.	B
2.	B		12.	D
3.	B		13.	A
4.	A		14.	D
5.	D		15.	D
6.	A		16.	B
7.	D		17.	C
8.	E		18.	D
9.	A		19.	A
10.	E		20.	B

21. D
22. C
23. C
24. D
25. C

TEST 4

DIRECTIONS: Each question or incomplete statement is followed by several suggested answers or completions. Select the one that BEST answers the question or completes the statement. *PRINT THE LETTER OF THE CORRECT ANSWER IN THE SPACE AT THE RIGHT.*

1. A medically trained person who treats mental diseases is called a(n)
   A. psychologist   B. sociologist   C. psychiatrist
   D. physiologist   E. opthamologist

2. Of the following social agencies, the which must rely MOST on short-contact interviewing is the
   A. child-guidance clinic   B. Travelers' Aid Society
   C. Social Service Exchange   D. Hospital for Crippled Children
   E. juvenile court

3. The organization which has as one of its primary functions the mitigation of suffering caused by famine, fire, floods, and other national calamities is the
   A. National Safety Council   B. Salvation Army
   C. Public Administration Services   D. American National Red Cross
   E. American Legion

4. The MAIN difference between public welfare and private social agencies is that in public agencies
   A. case records are open to the public
   B. the granting of assistance cannot be sufficiently flexible to meet the varying needs of individual recipients
   C. only financial assistance may be provided
   D. all policies and procedures must be based upon statutory authorizations
   E. economical and efficient administration are stressed because their funds are obtained through public taxation

5. Proper handling of a case in which the applicant requires temporary congregate care would involve a referral initially to
   A. a private agency   B. a religious institution
   C. the state welfare agency   D. the federal government
   E. one of the municipal shelters

6. A recipient of relief who is in need of the services on an attorney but is unable to pay the customary fees, should generally be referred to the
   A. Small Claims Court   B. Domestic Relations Court
   C. County Lawyers Association   D. City Law Department
   E. Legal Aid Society

7. A person who is not satisfied with the action taken by the Department of Social Services on his application for old-age assistance may appeal to the State Department of Social Welfare for an impartial review and a *fair hearing*.

The final decision in such a hearing is made by the
- A. State Board of Social Welfare
- B. State Commissioner of Social Welfare
- C. Commissioner of Social Services
- D. Attorney-General of the State
- E. Federal Security Agency

8. An injured worker should file his claim for workmen's compensation with the
    - A. State Labor Relations Board
    - B. Division of Placement and Unemployment Insurance
    - C. State Industrial Commission
    - D. Workmen's Compensation Board
    - E. State Insurance Board

9. In order to supplement the care and guidance furnished to young people by the family and other social institutions, the legislature created a temporary agency known as the State Youth Commission.
Among the powers and duties of this Commission are those listed below, with the EXCEPTION of
    - A. supervising the administration of state institutions for juvenile delinquents
    - B. authorizing payment of state aid to municipalities in accordance with the provisions of the Youth Commission Act
    - C. making studies and recommendations regarding the guidance and treatment of juvenile delinquents
    - D. devising plans for the creation and operation of youth bureaus and recreation projects
    - E. making necessary studies and analyses of the problems of youth guidance and the prevention of juvenile delinquency

10. One of the institutions operated by the State Department of Social Welfare is the
    - A. State School for the Blind, Batavia
    - B. State Training School for Boys, Warwick
    - C. State Reconstruction Home, West Haverstraw
    - D. State School for Mental Defectives, Newark
    - E. Woodbourne Institute for Defective Delinquents, Woodbourne

11. The one of the following which is NOT included among the responsibilities of the Bureau of Public Assistance of the Social Security Administration is
    - A. reviewing and approving state plans for public assistance and the operation of these plans, in order to determine their continuing conformity to the Social Security Act
    - B. administering provisions for grants by the federal government to states for old-age assistance, aid to the blind, aid to dependent children, and aid to the permanently and totally disabled
    - C. carrying out the Social Security Administration's functions in connection with the federal-state unemployment insurance system

3 (#4)

D. reviewing state estimates for public assistance and certifying the amount of federal grants to states
E. collecting, analyzing, and publishing data on the operation of all forms of public assistance in the states, including general assistance

12. Because of the number of able-bodied employable persons on relief, the Department of Social Services once adopted the policy of
    A. removing all employables from the relief rolls
    B. subjecting such persons to special review in order to determine whether they are concealing facts about employment
    C. assigning such persons to various city departments for appropriate employment commensurate with the amount of relief grants
    D. forcing all men on the employable list to apply to other governmental agencies as provisional civil service workers
    E. requesting selective service boards to give preference to such employable persons of appropriate age for induction into the armed forces

12.____

13. The type of insurance found MOST frequently among families such as those assisted by the Department of Social Services is
    A. accident   B. straight life   C. endowment
    D. industrial   E. personal liability

13.____

14. Of the following items in the standard budget of the Department of Social Services, the one for which actual expenditures would be MOST constant throughout the year is
    A. fuel   B. housing
    C. medical care   D. clothing
    E. household replacements

14.____

15. The MOST frequent cause of *broken homes* is attributed to the
    A. temperamental incompatibilities of parents and in-laws
    B. extension of the system of children's courts
    C. psychopathic irresponsibility of the parents
    D. institutionalization of one of the spouses
    E. death of one or both spouses

15.____

16. In rearing children, the problems of the widower are usually greater than those of the widow, largely because of the
    A. tendency of widowers to impose excessively rigid moral standards
    B. increased economic hardship
    C. added difficulty of maintaining a desirable home
    D. possibility that a stepmother will be added to the household
    E. prevalent masculine prejudice against pursuits which are inherently feminine

16.____

17. Foster-home placement of children is often advocated in preference to institutionalization PRIMARILY because
    A. the law does not provide for local supervision of children's institutions
    B. institutions furnish a more expensive type of care
    C. the number of institutions is insufficient compared to the number of children needing car
    D. children are not well treated in institutions
    E. foster homes provide a more normal environment for children

18. Of the following, the category MOST likely to yield the greatest reduction in cost to the taxpayer under improved employment conditions is
    A. home relief, including aid to the homeless
    B. aid to the blind
    C. aid to dependent children
    D. old-age assistance
    E. aid to the permanently and totally disabled

19. One of the MOST common characteristics of the chronic alcoholic is
    A. low intelligence level
    B. wanderlust
    C. psychosis
    D. independence
    E. egocentricity

20. Of the following factors leading toward the cure of the alcoholic, the MOST important is thought to be
    A. removal of all alcohol from the immediate environment
    B. development of a sense of personal adequacy
    C. social disapproval of drinking
    D. segregation from former companions
    E. intensive supervision by parole officers

21. An interview is BEST conducted in private primarily because
    A. the person interviewed will tend to be less self-conscious
    B. the interviewer will be able to maintain his continuity of thought better
    C. it will insure that the interview is *off the record*
    D. people tend to *show off* before an audience
    E. constant interruption by visitors and telephone calls will irritate the interviewer

22. An interviewer will be better able to understand the person interviewed and his problems if he recognizes that much of the person's behavior is due to motives
    A. which are deliberate
    B. of which he is unaware
    C. which are inexplicable
    D. which are kept under control
    E. which are calculated to deceive

23. When an applicant for public assistance is repeatedly told that *everything will be all right*, the effect that can usually be expected is that he will
    A. develop overt negativistic reactions toward the agency
    B. become too closely identified with the interviewer

C. doubt the interviewer's ability to understand and help with his problems
D. have greater confidence in the interviewer
E. make no appreciable change in his attitude toward the interviewer

24. While interviewing a client, it is preferable that the social service worker
    A. take no notes in order to avoid disturbing the client
    B. focus primary attention on the client while the client is talking
    C. take no notes in order to impress upon the client the worker's ability to remember all the pertinent facts of his case
    D. record all details in order to show the client that what he says is important
    E. record all details in order to impress upon the client the official character of his statements

25. During an interview, a curious applicant asks several questions about the social service worker's private life.
    As the interviewer, you should
    A. refuse to answer such questions
    B. answer his questions fully
    C. explain that your primary concern is with his problems and that discussion of your personal affairs will not be helpful in meeting his needs
    D. explain that it is the responsibility of the interviewer to ask questions and not to answer them
    E. answer only enough of his questions to the extent necessary to establish a friendly relationship with him

KEY (CORRECT ANSWERS)

1. C
2. B
3. D
4. D
5. E

6. E
7. B
8. D
9. A
10. B

11. C
12. C
13. D
14. B
15. E

16. C
17. E
18. A
19. E
20. B

21. A
22. B
23. C
24. C
25. C

TEST 5

DIRECTIONS: Each question or incomplete statement is followed by several suggested answers or completions. Select the one that BEST answers the question or completes the statement. *PRINT THE LETTER OF THE CORRECT ANSWER IN THE SPACE AT THE RIGHT.*

1. An interviewer can BEST establish a good relationship with the person being interviewed by
   A. assuming casual interest in the statements made by the person being interviewed
   B. asking questions which enable the person to show pride in his knowledge
   C. taking the point of view of the person interviewed
   D. controlling the interview to a major extent
   E. showing a genuine interest in the person

   1._____

2. An interviewer's attention must be directed toward himself as well as toward the person interviewed.
   This statement means that the interviewer should
   A. keep in mind the extent to which his own prejudices may influence his judgment
   B. rationalize the statements made by the person interviewed
   C. gain the respect and confidence of the person interviewed
   D. avoid being too impersonal
   E. avoid using indirect methods in eliciting information from the person interviewed

   2._____

3. More complete expression will be obtained from a person being interviewed if the interviewer can create the impression that
   A. the data secured will become part of a permanent record
   B. official information must be accurate in every detail
   C. it is the duty of the person interviewed to give accurate data
   D. the interviewer checks additional sources to get complete data
   E. the person interviewed is participating in a discussion of his own problems

   3._____

4. The practice of asking leading questions should be avoided in an interview because the
   A. interviewer risks revealing his attitudes to the person being interviewed
   B. interviewer may be led to ignore the objective attitudes of the person interviewed
   C. answers may be unwarrantedly influenced
   D. person interviewed will resent the attempt to lead him and will be less cooperative
   E. replies to such questions are always verbose

   4._____

5. A good technique for the interviewer to use in an effort to secure reliable data and to reduce the possibility of misunderstanding is to
   A. use casual undirected conversation, enabling the person being interviewed to talk about himself, and thus secure the desired information
   B. adopt the procedure of using direct questions regularly
   C. extract the desired information from the person being interviewed by putting him on the defensive
   D. explain to the person being interviewed the information desired and the reason for needing it
   E. explain that he is an experienced interviewer and can detect false statements

6. As a social service worker interviewing an applicant for public assistance, your attitude toward his veracity should be that the information he has furnished you is
   A. *untruthful* until you have had an opportunity to check the information
   B. *truthful* only insofar as verifiable facts are concerned
   C. *untruthful* because clients tend to interpret everything in their own favor
   D. *truthful* until you have information to the contrary
   E. *untruthful* because most applicants are unreliable

7. When a public assistance agency assigns its most experienced interviewers to conduct initial interviews with applicants, the MOST important reason for its action is that
   A. experienced workers are always older, and therefore command the respect of applicants
   B. the applicant may be given a complete understanding of the procedures to be followed and the time involved in obtaining assistance payments
   C. applicants with fraudulent intentions will be detected, and prevented from obtaining further services from the agency
   D. the agency may immediately obtain an accurate and complete plan to be followed in giving assistance to the applicant
   E. the applicant may be given an understanding of the purpose of the assistance program and of the bases for granting assistance, in addition to the routine information

8. As a social service worker conducting the first interview with an applicant for public assistance, you should
   A. ask questions requiring *yes* or *no* answers in order to simplify the interview
   B. rephrase several of the key questions as a check on his previous statements
   C. let him tell his own story while keeping him to the relevant facts
   D. avoid showing any sympathy for the applicant while he is revealing his personal needs and problems
   E. ask only direct questions so as to demonstrate your impersonal approach

9. An aged person who is unable to produce immediate proof of age has made an application for old-age assistance. He states that it will take about a week to obtain the necessary proof and that he does not have enough money to provide meals for himself until then.
   If it appears that he is in immediate need, he should be told that
   A. the law requires proof of age before any assistance can be granted
   B. temporary assistance will be provided pending the completion of the investigation
   C. a personal loan will be provided from a revolving fund
   D. he should arrange for a small loan from private sources
   E. he will have to produce an affidavit witnessed by two relatives who will vouch for the accuracy of his statements before any assistance can be provided

10. If the social service worker learns during the interview that the client has applied for public assistance without the knowledge of her husband, even though he is a member of the same household, the worker should
    A. appear not to notice this oversight, but watch for other evidences of marital discord
    B. make no mention of this to the applicant, but before taking final action send a note to the husband asking him to come in
    C. discuss this situation with the client and help her recognize the value of her husband's participation in the application
    D. point out to the applicant the implications of her behavior and ask for an explanation of her motives
    E. tell the applicant that the husband's needs will be excluded from the budget until he appears for a personal interview

11. Responsibility for fully informing the public about the availability of public assistance can MOST successfully be discharged by
    A. local public assistance agencies   B. social service exchanges
    C. community chest organizations   D. councils of social agencies
    E. service clubs

12. Of the sources through which a welfare agency can seek information about the family background and economic needs of a particular client, the MOST important consists of
    A. records and documents covering the client
    B. interviews with the client's relatives
    C. the client's own story
    D. direct contacts with former employers
    E. information offered by the client's neighbors

13. The one of the following sources of evidence which would MOST likely to give information needed to verify residence is
    A. family affidavits   B. medical and hospital bills
    C. an original birth certificate D. rental receipts
    E. an insurance policy

14. In public assistance agencies, vital statistics are a resource used by the workers MAINLY to
    A. help establish eligibility through verification of births, deaths, and marriages
    B. help establish eligibility through verification of divorce proceedings
    C. secure proof of unemployment and eligibility for unemployment compensation
    D. secure indices of the cost of living in the larger cities
    E. discourage applications from ineligible persons

15. Case record should be considered confidential in order to
    A. make it impossible for agencies to know each other's methods
    B. permit worker to make objective rather than subjective comments
    C. prevent recipients from comparing amounts of assistance given to different families
    D. keep pertinent information from other social workers
    E. protect clients and their families

16. Because the social service worker generally is not trained as a psychiatrist, he should, when encountering psychiatric problems in the performance of his departmental duties,
    A. ignore such problems because they are beyond the scope of his responsibilities
    B. inform the affected persons that he recognizes their problems personally but will take no official cognizance of them
    C. ask to be relieved of the cases in which these problems are met and recommend that they be assigned to a psychiatrist
    D. recognize such problems where they exist and make referrals to the proper sources for treatment
    E. ask his supervisor to assign a psychiatric case worker to accompany him on all subsequent visits to the client

17. The family budget is a device used by the Department of Social Services to
    A. determine changes in the cost-of-living index
    B. estimate the needs of families and the amount of assistance necessary to meet this needs
    C. evaluate its financial condition
    D. estimate probable expenditures during a given period
    E. determine whether an applicant is eligible for categorical assistance or for general relief

18. The amount included for food for each client in Department of Social Services budgets should
    A. be based on quantitative caloric estimates of energy requirements rather than on variety in the kinds of foods
    B. be high enough to provide minimum subsistence, but low enough to discourage ineligible applicants
    C. exclude special dietary needs which are relatively expensive

D. cover food idiosyncrasies of various members of the household
E. meet the generally accepted standards for proper nutrition

19. The program for aid to dependent children is PRIMARILY directed toward 19._____
    A. the placement and supervision of children in selected foster homes
    B. provision of assistance whereby children can remain in their own homes or in the homes of relatives
    C. rehabilitation of neglected and delinquent children
    D. provision of specialized services to children in areas of special need
    E. provision of assistance to widows of good moral character for the care of their children

20. Since need is a condition of eligibility in the old-age assistance program, an assistance payment to an aged recipient should be based upon a consideration of 20._____
    A. the length of time he received general relief prior to his application for old-age assistance
    B. his attitude toward the agency
    C. his total needs and resources
    D. the probable duration of his dependency
    E. the average monthly cost of institutional care

21. From a social point of view, the reason for the growth of the practice of giving public assistance in the form of cash payments is the 21._____
    A. resultant reduction in complaints coming to the agency
    B. increased necessity for developing nationwide comparative statistics
    C. facilitation of recovery for relief improperly granted
    D. public's increasing belief in the essential justice of this type of assistance

22. In closing the case of a client, the social service worker should attempt to give the client a(n) 22._____
    A. feeling of being rejected by the agency as a worthy person
    B. idea of the progress of similar cases being handled by the agency
    C. understanding that his case could be reopened for full relief, if necessary, but not for emergency assistance
    D. explanation of the conditions upon which he might make re-application
    E. explanation of the limitations of the agency in meeting his needs

23. There is widespread agreement among nearly all planning groups concerned with public assistance that 23._____
    A. need for public assistance should be the primary, if not the only, condition of eligibility; and that all arbitrary conditions of eligibility such as citizenship, ownership of home, and moral character should be eliminated from all public assistance programs
    B. public assistance grants should be paid by voucher rather than in cash because most recipients do not use cash allowances for the purposes for which they are intended
    C. the names of persons receiving public assistance should be publicized in order to prevent fraud

D. public assistance should be discontinued immediately whenever the unemployed father of a family receiving assistance refuses a job offer
E. public assistance should not be provided for any persons who own property or who have any financial resources

24. Of fundamental importance to the work of social worker in the Department of Social Services is
    A. the knowledge of when to use the power of the Department to subdue an angry client
    B. an ability to classify clients according to common characteristics as described in case records
    C. the ability to explain eligibility in terms of legal requirements with clarity and simplicity
    D. the realization that persons who apply for public assistance have become independent because of lack of industriousness and are therefore unable to manage their own affairs
    E. a general knowledge of the executive, administrative, and supervisory functions of the Department

25. Although a social worker in the Department of Social Services has several responsibilities, his PRIMARY one is to
    A. nullify any restrictive rules and regulations issued by the State Department of Social Welfare
    B. carry out his own interpretation of the function of the Department of Social Services
    C. carry out the objectives of Department of Social Services programs as set forth in the Social Welfare Law
    D. avoid community criticism of the manner in which the programs of the Department of Social Services are conducted
    E. give relief to all applicants who claim they are eligible

KEY (CORRECT ANSWERS)

1.	E		11.	A
2.	A		12.	C
3.	E		13.	D
4.	C		14.	A
5.	D		15.	E
6.	D		16.	D
7.	E		17.	B
8.	C		18.	E
9.	B		19.	B
10.	C		20.	C

21.	D
22.	D
23.	A
24.	C
25.	C

EXAMINATION SECTION
TEST 1

DIRECTIONS: Each question or incomplete statement is followed by several suggested answers or completions. Select the one that BEST answers the question or completes the statement. *PRINT THE LETTER OF THE CORRECT ANSWER IN THE SPACE AT THE RIGHT.*

1. When a worker is planning a future interview with a client, of the following, the MOST important consideration is the
   A. recommendations he will make to the client
   B. place where the client will be interviewed
   C. purpose for which the client will be interviewed
   D. personality of the client

   1.____

2. For a worker to make a practice of reviewing the client's case record, if available, prior to the interview is usually
   A. *inadvisable*, because knowledge of the client's past record will tend to influence the worker's judgment
   B. *advisable*, because knowledge of the client's background will help the worker to identify discrepancies in the client's responses
   C. *inadvisable*, because such review is time-consuming and of questionable value
   D. *advisable*, because knowledge of the client's background will help the worker to understand the client's situation

   2.____

3. Assume that a worker makes a practice of constantly re-assuring clients with serious and complex problems by making such statements as: *I'm sure you'll soon be well; I know you'll get a job soon*; or *Everything will be all right.*
   Of the following, the MOST likely result of such practice is to
   A. encourage the client and make him feel that the worker understands what the client is going through
   B. make the client doubtful about the worker's understanding of his difficulties and the worker's ability to help
   C. confuse the client and cause him to hesitate to take any action on his own initiative
   D. help the client to be more realistic about his situation and the probability that it will improve

   3.____

4. In order to get the maximum amount of information from a client during an interview, of the following, it is MOST important for the worker to communicate to the client the feeling that the worker is
   A. interested in the client
   B. a figure of authority
   C. efficient in his work habits
   D. sympathetic to the client's lifestyle

   4.____

5. Of the following, the worker who takes extremely detailed notes during an interview with a client is MOST likely to
   A. encourage the client to talk freely
   B. distract and antagonize the client
   C. help the client feel at ease
   D. understand the client's feelings

6. You find that many of the clients you interview are verbally abusive and unusually hostile to you.
   Of the following, the MOST appropriate action for you to take FIRST is to
   A. review your interviewing techniques and consider whether you may be provoking these clients
   B. act in a more authoritative manner when interviewing troublesome clients
   C. tell these clients that you will not process their applications unless their troublesome behavior ceases
   D. disregard the clients' troublesome behavior during the interviews

7. During an interview, you did not completely understand several of your client's responses. In each instance, you rephrased the client's statement and asked the client if that was what he meant.
   For you to use such a technique during interviews would be considered
   A. *inappropriate*; you may have distorted the client's meaning by rephrasing his statements
   B. *inappropriate*; you should have asked the same question until you received a comprehensible response
   C. *appropriate*; the client will have a chance to correct you if you have misinterpreted his responses
   D. *appropriate*; a worker should rephrase clients' responses for the records

8. A worker is interviewing a client who has just had a severe emotional shock because of an assault on her by a mugger.
   Of the following, the approach which would generally be MOST helpful to the client is for the worker to
   A. comfort the client and encourage her to talk about the assault
   B. sympathize with the client but refuse to talk about the assault
   C. tell the client to control her emotions and think positively about the future
   D. proceed with the interview in an impersonal and unemotional manner

9. A worker finds that her questions are misinterpreted by many of the clients she interviews.
   Of the following, the MOST likely reason for this problem is that the
   A. client is not listening attentively
   B. client wants to avoid the subject being discussed
   C. worker has failed to express her meaning clearly
   D. worker has failed to put the client at ease

10. For a worker to look directly at the client and observe him during the interview is, generally,
    A. *inadvisable*; this will make the client nervous and uncomfortable
    B. *advisable*; the client will be more likely to refrain from lying
    C. *inadvisable*; the worker will not be able to take notes for the case record
    D. *advisable*; this will encourage conversation and accelerate the progress of the interview

10.____

11. You are interviewing a client who is applying for social services for the first time. In order to encourage this client to freely give you the information needed for you to establish his eligibility, of the following, the BEST way to start the interview is by
    A. asking questions the client can easily answer
    B. conveying the impression that his responses to your questions will be checked
    C. asking two or three similar but important questions
    D. assuring the client that your sole responsibility is *getting the facts*

11.____

12. Workers are encouraged to record significant information obtained from clients and services provided for clients.
    Of the following, the MOST important reason for this practice is that these case records will
    A. help to reduce the need for regular supervisory conferences
    B. indicate to workers which clients are taking up the most time
    C. provide information which will help the agency to improve its services to clients
    D. make it easier to verify the complaints of clients

12.____

13. As a worker in the employment eligibility section, you find that interviews can be completed in a shorter period of time if you ask questions which limit the client to a certain answer.
    For you to use such a technique would be considered
    A. *inappropriate*, because this type of question usually requires advance preparation
    B. *inappropriate*, because this type of question may inhibit the client from saying what he really means
    C. *appropriate*, because you know the areas into which the questions should be directed
    D. *appropriate*, because this type of question usually helps clients to express themselves clearly

13.____

14. Assume that a worker at a juvenile detention center is planning foster care placement for a child.
    For the worker to have the child participate in the planning is generally considered to be
    A. time-consuming and of little practical value in preparing the child for placement
    B. valuable in helping the child adjust to future placement

14.____

C. useful, because the child will be more likely to cooperate with others in the center
D. anxiety-provoking because the child will feel that he has been abandoned

15. You have been assigned to interview the mother of a five-year-old son in her home to get information useful in locating the child's absent father. During the interview, you notice many serious bruises on the child's arms and legs, which the mother explains are due to the child's clumsiness.
Of the following, your BEST course of action is to
    A. accept the mother's explanation and concentrate on getting information which will help you to locate the father
    B. advise the mother to have the child examined for a medical condition that may be causing his clumsiness
    C. make a surprise visit to the mother later, to see whether someone is beating the child
    D. complete your interview with the mother and report the case to your supervisor for investigation of possible child abuse

16. During an interview, the former landlord of an absent father offers to help you to locate the father if you will give the landlord confidential information you have on the financial situation of the father.
Of the following, you should
    A. immediately end the interview with the landlord
    B. urge the landlord to help you but explain that you are not permitted to give him confidential information
    C. freely give the landlord the confidential information he requests about the father
    D. give the landlord the information only if he promises to keep it confidential

17. You feel that your client, a released mental patient, is not adjusting well to living on his own in an apartment. To gather more information, you interview privately his next-door neighbor, who claims that the client is creating a disturbance and speaks of the client in an angry and insulting manner.
Of the following, the BEST action for you to take in this situation is to
    A. listen patiently to the neighbor to try to get the facts about your client's behavior
    B. inform the neighbor that he has no right to speak insultingly about a mentally ill person
    C. make an appointment to interview the neighbor some other time when he isn't so upset
    D. tell the neighbor that you were not aware of the client's behavior and that you will have the client moved

18. As a worker assigned to an income maintenance center, you are interviewing a client to determine his eligibility for a work program. Suddenly, the client begins to shout that he is in no condition to work and that you are persecuting him for no reason.

Of the following, your BEST response to this client is to
- A. advise the client to stop shouting or you will call for the security guard
- B. wait until the client calms down, then order him to come back for another interview
- C. insist that you are not persecuting the client and that he must complete the interview
- D. wait until the client calms down, say that you understand how he feels, and try to continue the interview

19. You are counseling a mother whose 17-year-old son has recently been returned home from a mental institution. Although she is willing to care for her son at home, she is frightened by his strange and sometimes violent behavior and does not know the best arrangement to make for his care.
Of the following, your MOST appropriate response to this mother's problem is to
    - A. describe the supportive services and alternatives to home care which are available
    - B. help her to accept her son's strange and violent behavior
    - C. tell her that she will not be permitted to care for her son at home if she is frightened by his behavior
    - D. convince her that she is not responsible for her son's mental condition

20. Assume that, as an intake worker, you are interviewing an elderly man who comes to the center several times a month to discuss topics with you which are not related to social service. You realize that the man is lonely and enjoys these conversations.
Of the following, it would be MOST appropriate to
    - A. politely discourage the man from coming in to pass the time with you
    - B. avoid speaking to this man the next time he comes into the center
    - C. explore with the client his feelings about joining a Senior Citizens' Center
    - D. continue to hold these conversations with the man

21. A client you are interviewing in the housing elibility section tends to ramble on after each response that he gives, so that man clients are kept waiting.
In this situation, of the following, it would be MOST advisable to
    - A. try to direct the interview, in order to obtain the necessary information
    - B. reduce the number of questions asked so that you can shorten the interview
    - C. arrange a second interview for the client so that you can give him more time
    - D. tell the client that he is wasting everybody's time

22. A non-minority worker in an employment eligibility unit is about to interview a minority client on public assistance for job placement when the client says:
What does your kind know about my problems? You've never had to survive out on these streets.
Of the following, the worker's MOST appropriate response to this situation is to

A. postpone the interview until a minority worker is available to interview the client
B. tell the client that he must cooperate with the worker if he wants to continue receiving public assistance
C. explain to the client the function of the worker in this unit and the services he provides
D. assure the client that you do not have to be a member of a minority group to understand the effects of poverty

23. As a worker in a family services unit, you have been assigned to follow-up a case folder recently forwarded from the protective-diagnostic unit.
After making appropriate clerical notations in your records such as name of client and date of receipt, which of the following would be the MOST appropriate step to take next?
A. Confer with your supervisor
B. Read and review all reports included in the case folder
C. Arrange to visit with the client at his home
D. Confer with representatives of any other agencies which have been in contact with the client

23.____

24. As a worker in the employment section, you are interviewing a young client who seriously underestimates the amount of education and training he will require for a certain occupation.
For you to tell the client that you think he is mistaken would, generally, be considered
A. *inadvisable*, because workers should not express their opinions to clients
B. *inadvisable*, because clients have the right to self-determination
C. *advisable*, because clients should generally be alerted to their misconceptions
D. *advisable*, because workers should convince clients to adopt a proper lifestyle

25.____

25. As an intake worker, you are counseling a mother and her unmarried, thirteen-year-old daughter, who is six months pregnant, concerning the advisability of placing the daughter's baby for adoption. The mother insists on adoption, but the daughter remains silent and appears undecided.
Of the following, you should encourage the daughter to
A. make the final decision on adoption herself
B. keep her baby despite her mother's insistence on adoption
C. accept her mother's insistence on adoption
D. make the decision on adoption together with her mother

25.____

KEY (CORRECT ANSWERS)

1.	C	11.	A
2.	D	12.	C
3.	B	13.	B
4.	A	14.	B
5.	B	15.	D
6.	A	16.	B
7.	C	17.	A
8.	A	18.	D
9.	C	19.	A
10.	D	20.	C

21. A
22. C
23. B
24. C
25. D

TEST 2

DIRECTIONS: Each question or incomplete statement is followed by several suggested answers or completions. Select the one that BEST answers the question or completes the statement. *PRINT THE LETTER OF THE CORRECT ANSWER IN THE SPACE AT THE RIGHT.*

1. You are interviewing a legally responsible absent father who refuses to make child support payments because he claims the mother physically abuses the child.
   Of the following, the BEST way for you to handle his situation is to tell the father that you
   A. will report his complaint about the mother, but he is still responsible for making child support payments
   B. suspect that he is complaining about the mother in order to avoid his own responsibility for making child support payments
   C. are concerned with his responsibility to make child support payments, not with the mother's abuse of the child
   D. cannot determine his responsibility for making child support payments until his complaint about the mother is investigated

2. On a visit to a home where child abuse is alleged, you find the mother preparing lunch for her two children. She tells you that she knows that a neighbor is spreading lies about her treatment of the children.
   Which one of the following is the BEST action for you to take?
   A. Thank the mother for her assistance, leave the home, and indicate in your report that the allegation of child abuse is false
   B. Tell the mother that, since you have been sent to visit her, there must be some truth to the allegations
   C. Explain the purpose of your visit and observe whatever interaction takes place between the children and the mother
   D. Conclude the interview, since you have observed the mother preparing a good lunch for the children

3. You are interviewing an elderly woman who lives alone to determine her eligibility for homemaker service at public expense. Though obviously frail and in need of this service, the woman is not completely cooperative, and, during the interview, is often silent for a considerable period of time.
   Of the following, the BEST way for you to deal with these periods of silence is to
   A. realize that she may be embarrassed to have to apply for homemaker service at public expense, and emphasize her right to this service
   B. postpone the interview and make an appointment with her for a later date, when she may be better able to cooperate
   C. explain to the woman that you have many clients to interview and need her cooperation to complete the interview quickly
   D. recognize that she is probably hiding something and begin to ask questions to draw her out

2 (#2)

4. During a conference with an adolescent boy at a juvenile detention center, you find out for the first time that he would prefer to be placed in foster care rather than return to his natural parents.
To uncover the reasons why the boy dislikes his own home, of the following, it would be MOST advisable for you to
   A. ask the boy a number of short, simple questions about his feelings
   B. encourage the boy to talk freely and express his feelings as best he can
   C. interview the parents and find out why the boy doesn't want to live at home
   D. administer a battery of psychological tests in order to make an assessment of the boy's problems

1._____

5. Of the following, the BEST way to determine which activities should be provided for members of a Senior Citizens' Center is to
   A. ask the neighborhood community board to submit their recommendations
   B. meet with the professional staff of the center to get their opinions
   C. encourage the members of the center to express their personal preferences
   D. study the schedules prepared by other Senior Citizens' Centers for guidance

5._____

6. You are interviewing a mother who is applying for Aid to Families with Dependent Children because the husband has deserted the family. The mother becomes annoyed at having to answer your questions and tells you to leave her apartment.
Which one of the following actions would be MOST appropriate to take FIRST in this situation?
   A. Return to the office and close the case for lack of cooperation
   B. Tell the mother that you will get the information from her neighbors if she does not cooperate
   C. Tell the mother that you must stay until you get answers to your questions
   D. Explain to the mother the reasons for the interview and the consequences of her failure to cooperate

6._____

7. A worker assigned to visit homebound clients to determine their eligibility for Medicaid must understand each client's situation as completely as possible.
Of the following source which may provide insight into the client's situation, the one that is generally MOST revealing is:
   A. Close relatives of the client, who have known him for many years
   B. Next-door neighbors, who have observed the daily living habits of the client
   C. The client himself, who can provide his own description of his situation
   D. The records of other social agencies that may have served the client

7._____

8. A worker counseling juvenile clients finds that, although he can tolerate most of their behavior, he becomes infuriated when they lie to him.
Of the following, the worker can BEST deal with his anger at his clients' lying by

8._____

63

A. recognizing his feelings of anger and learning to control expression of these feelings to his clients
B. warning his clients that he cannot be responsible for his anger when a client lies to him
C. using willpower to suppress his feelings of anger when a client lies to him
D. realizing that lying is a common trait of juveniles and not directed against him personally

9. During an interview at the employment eligibility section, one of your clients, a former drug addict, has expressed an interest in attending a community counseling center and resuming his education.
In this case, the MOST appropriate action that you should take FIRST is to
   A. determine whether this ambition is realistic for a former drug addict
   B. send the client's application to a community counseling center which provides services to former addicts
   C. ask the client whether he is really motivated or is just seeking your approval
   D. encourage and assist the client to take this step, since his interest is a positive sign

10. Because of habitual neglect by his mother, a five-year-old boy has been placed in a foster home.
For the worker to encourage the mother to visit the boy in the foster home is, generally,
   A. *desirable*, because the boy will be helped by continuing his ties with his mother
   B. *undesirable*, because the boy will be upset by his mother's visits and will have a harder time adjusting to the foster home
   C. *desirable*, because the mother will learn from the foster parents how she should treat the boy
   D. *undesirable*, because the mother should be punished for her neglect of the boy by complete separation from him

11. You are interviewing a client who, during previous appointments, has not responded to your requests for information required to determine his continued eligibility for services. On this occasion, the client again offers an excuse which you feel is not acceptable.
For you to advise the client of the probable loss of services because of his lack of cooperation is
   A. *inappropriate*, because the threat to withhold services will harm the relationship between worker and client
   B. *inappropriate*, because workers should not reveal to clients that they do not believe their statements
   C. *appropriate*, because social services are a reward given to cooperative clients
   D. *appropriate*, because the worker should inform clients of the consequences of their lack of cooperation

4 (#2)

12. Assume that you are counseling an adolescent boy in a juvenile detention center who has been a ringleader in smuggling pot into the center.
During your regular interview with this boy, of the following, it would be *advisable* to
    A. tell him you know that he has been involved in smuggling pot and that you are trying to understand the reasons for his misbehavior
    B. ignore his pot smuggling in order to reassure him that you understand and accept him, even though you do not agree with his standards of behavior
    C. warn him that you have reported his pot smuggling and that he will be punished for his misbehavior
    D. show him that you disagree of his pot smuggling, but assure him that you will not report him for his misbehavior

12.____

13. Your unit has received several complaints about a homeless elderly woman living outdoors in various locations in the area. To help determine the need for protective services for this woman, you interview several persons in the neighborhood who are familiar with her, but all are uncooperative or reluctant to give information.
Of the following, your BEST approach to these persons is to explain to them that
    A. you will take legal steps against them if they do not cooperate with you
    B. their cooperation may enable you to help this homeless woman
    C. you need their cooperation to remove this homeless woman from their neighborhood
    D. they will be responsible for any harm that comes to this homeless woman

13.____

14. A foster mother complains to the worker that a ten-year-old boy placed with her is overaggressive and unmanageable. The worker, knowing that the boy has been placed unsuccessfully several times before, constantly reassures the foster mother that the boy is improving steadily.
For the worker to do this, generally,
    A. *good practice*, because the foster mother may accept the professional opinion of the worker and keep the boy
    B. *poor practice*, because the foster mother may be discouraged from discussing the boy's problems with the worker
    C. *good practice*, because the foster mother may feel guilty if she gives up the boy when he is improving
    D. *poor practice*, because the boy should not remain with a foster mother who complains about his behavior

14.____

15. Assume that, as a worker in the liaison and adjustment unit, you are interviewing a client regarding an adjustment in budget. The client begins to scream at you that she holds you responsible for the decrease in her allowance.
Of the following, which is the BEST way for you to handle this situation?
    A. Attempt to discuss the matter calmly with the client and explain her right to a hearing
    B. Urge the client to appeal and assure her of your support

15.____

C. Tell the client that her disorderly behavior will be held against her
D. Tell the client that the reduction is due to red tape and is not your fault

16. As a worker assigned to a juvenile detention center, you are having a counseling interview with a recently admitted boy who is having serious problems in adjusting to confinement in the center. During the interview, the boy frequently interrupts to ask you personal questions.
Of the following, the BEST way for you to deal with these questions is to
   A. tell him in a friendly way that your job is to discuss his problems, not yours
   B. try to understand how the questions relate to the boy's own problems and reply with discretion
   C. take no notice of the questions and continue with the interview
   D. try to win the boy's confidence by answering his questions in detail

17. A worker is interviewing an elderly woman who hesitates to provide necessary information about her finances to determine whether she is eligible for supplementary assistance. She fears that this information will be reported to others and that her neighbors will find out that she is destitute and applying for welfare.
Of the following, the worker's MOST appropriate response is to
   A. tell her that, if she hesitates to give this information, the agency will get it from other sources
   B. assure her that this information is kept strictly confidential, and will not be given to unauthorized persons
   C. convince her that her application will be turned down unless she provides this information as soon as possible
   D. ask for the name and address of her nearest relative and obtain the information from that person

18. You are counseling a couple whose children have been placed in a foster home because of the couple's quarrelling and child neglect. When you interview the wife by herself, she tells you that she knows the husband often cheats on her with other women, but she is too afraid of the husband's temper to tell him how much this hurts her.
For you to immediately reveal to the husband the wife's unhappiness concerning his cheating is, generally,
   A. *good practice*, because it will help the husband to understand why his wife quarrels with him
   B. *poor practice*, because information received from the wife should not be given to the husband without her permission
   C. *good practice*, because the husband will direct his anger at you rather than at his wife
   D. *poor practice*, because the wife may have told you a false story about her husband in order to win your sympathy

19. A worker in an employment eligibility section is beginning a job placement interview with a tall, strongly-built young man. As the man sits down, the worker comments: *I know a big fellow like you wouldn't be interested in any clerical job.*
For the worker to make such a comment is, generally,
    A. *appropriate*, because it creates an air of familiarity which may put the man at ease
    B. *inappropriate*, because the man may be sensitive about his physical size
    C. *appropriate*, because the worker is using his judgment to help speed up the interview
    D. *inappropriate*, because the man may feel he is being pressured into agreeing with the worker

20. Workers at a juvenile detention center are responsible for establishing constructive relationships with the youths confined to the center in order to help them adjust to detention.
Of the following, the BEST way for a worker to deal with a youth who acts over-aggressive and hostile is to
    A. take appropriate disciplinary measures
    B. attempt to distract the youth by encouraging him to engage in physical sports
    C. try to discover the real reasons for the youth's hostile behavior
    D. urge the youth to express his anger against the institution instead of *taking it out* on you

21. A worker in a men's shelter is counseling a middle-aged client for alcoholism. During counseling, the client confesses that, many years ago, he had often enjoyed sexually abusing his ten-year-old daughter. The worker tells the client that he personally finds the client's behavior *morally disgusting*.
For the worker to tell the client this is, generally,
    A. *acceptable counseling practice*, because it may encourage the client to feel guilty about his behavior
    B. *unacceptable counseling practice*, because the client may try to shock the worker by confessing other similar behavior
    C. *acceptable counseling practice*, because *letting off steam* in this manner may relieve tension between the worker and the client
    D. *unacceptable counseling practice*, because the client may hesitate to discuss his behavior frankly with the worker in the future

22. During your discussion with a foster mother who has had a nine-year-old boy in placement for about one month, you are told that the child is disruptive in school and has been unruly and hostile toward the foster family. The boy had been quiet and docile before placement.
In this situation, it would be MOST appropriate to suggest to the foster mother that
    A. this behavior is normal for a nine-year-old boy
    B. children placed in foster homes usually go through a period of testing their foster parents

C. the child must have picked up these patterns from the foster family
D. this behavior is probably a sign that she is too strict with the boy

23. During an interview in the housing eligibility section, your client, who wants to move to a larger apartment, asks you to decide on a suitable neighborhood for her.
For you, the worker, to make such a decision for the client would generally be considered
   A. *appropriate*, because you can save time and expense by sharing your knowledge of neighborhoods with the client
   B. *inappropriate*, because workers should not help clients with this type of decision
   C. *appropriate*, because this will help the client to develop confidence in her ability to make decisions
   D. *inappropriate*, because the client should be encouraged to accept the responsibility of making this decision

23.____

24. Your client, an elderly man left unable to care for himself after a stroke, has been referred for home-attendant services, but insists that he does not need these services. You believe that the man considers this to be an insult to his pride and that he will not allow himself to admit that he needs help.
Of the following, the MOST appropriate action for you to take is to
   A. withdraw the referral for home-attendant services and allow the client to try to take care of himself
   B. process the request for home-attendant services on the assumption that the client will soon realize that he cannot care for himself
   C. discuss with the client your interpretation of his problem and attempt to persuade him to accept home-attendant services
   D. tell the client that he will have no further opportunity to apply for home-attendant services if he does not accept them at this time

24.____

25. A worker making a field visit to investigate a complaint of child abuse finds that the parents of the child are a racially mixed couple. The child appears poorly dressed and unruly.
Of the following, the MOST appropriate approach for the worker to take in this situation is to
   A. take the child aside and ask him privately if either of his parents ever mistreats him
   B. determine if prejudice against the couple has led them to use the child as a scapegoat
   C. question the non-minority parent closely for signs of resentment of the child's mixed parentage
   D. observe the relationship between parents and child for indications of abuse by the parents

25.____

KEY (CORRECT ANSWERS)

1.	A	11.	D
2.	C	12.	A
3.	A	13.	B
4.	B	14.	B
5.	C	15.	A
6.	D	16.	B
7.	C	17.	B
8.	A	18.	B
9.	D	19.	D
10.	A	20.	C

21. D
22. B
23. D
24. C
25. D

EXAMINATION SECTION
TEST 1

DIRECTIONS: Each question or incomplete statement is followed by several suggested answers or completions. Select the one that BEST answers the question or completes the statement. *PRINT THE LETTER OF THE CORRECT ANSWER IN THE SPACE AT THE RIGHT.*

1. One day an elderly man asks you if he can apply for Social Security at the welfare office.
   Your response should be to
   A. tell him that it is foolish to think he can apply for Social Security at the welfare office
   B. take him back to his apartment because he is too old to be roaming the streets asking questions
   C. explain that Social Security is a federal program and direct him to the nearest Social Security office
   D. call his daughter and tell her that the family should take better care of their father

   1.____

2. One of your duties is to occasionally visit clients. On one occasion, you visit Mrs. B., who needs assistance in referral of her children for day care so that she may enter a job training program. She has postponed completing the referral.
   What should you do in this situation?
   A. Tell her that if she doesn't hurry there will be no room at the day care center and the training program will be closed
   B. Make the arrangements and tell Mrs. B. that she should do what you say
   C. Remember that all people who ask for help are not always ready to receive it and continue to allow Mrs. B. to complete the referral by herself
   D. The next time Mrs. B. asks for help, see that she gets it as slowly as possible

   2.____

3. Assume that you are trying to contact a community group to offer to meet with their representative to explain a new agency policy about intake procedures.
   In order to "get your message across," you should
   A. write a short concise letter explaining why you want to meet with them and when you will be available
   B. write a short letter stating only that it is important that they contact you in order to arrange a meeting
   C. ask a secretary to help you because you do not really like to write to groups
   D. call the agency rather than write since you know someone there

   3.____

4. It is necessary for you to call the director of a head start center in order to discuss 4.____
a training program for teaching aides. The operator asks who you are and
what you wish to discuss with the director.
Your response should be to
   A. tell her that you would rather explain to the director and you want to
      speak to her immediately
   B. identify yourself, your department, and the nature of your business with
      the director
   C. hang up and try to call again when another operator is on duty
   D. tell your supervisor that the operator at the head start center is rude and
      you would rather not be asked to call there again

5. Mr. A. wants her children to go to summer camp. She has receive the request 5.____
forms, but does not understand all of the questions and you are asked to help
her complete them. She comes to the office at the appointed time.
Of the following, the action you should take is to
   A. tell her she has taken so long that maybe the children will not go to camp
   B. see her as quickly as possible, explain the questions to her, and help her
      in completing the forms
   C. help her, but tell her she will have to learn to read better and refer her to
      an evening school
   D. fill out the forms or her by yourself

6. Mrs. B. needs a referral to the cancer clinic. You contact the clinic and make 6.____
arrangements for her visit. You go to her home to inform her about the time
because she has no phone. She thanks you for your help and then offers you
a piece of jewelry that appears to be rather expensive.
Of the following, the action you should take is to
   A. take the gift because you don't want to hurt her feelings
   B. tell her that she is foolish and should spend her money on herself
   C. explain to her that you are pleased with her thoughtfulness, but you are
      unable to accept the gift
   D. refuse the gift and get someone else to make referrals in the future
      because she is trying to pay you for your help

7. Mrs. C., a seemingly healthy, intelligent woman whose husband is disabled, and 7.____
who works part-time, asks for help in getting homemaker services.
Of the following, the action you should take is to
   A. give Mrs. C. the necessary information and help her get the services
   B. tell Mrs. C. that you do not feel she needs these services since her
      husband is capable of helping
   C. make note of her request since you do not feel it is urgent
   D. refer her to a caseworker since she obviously needs help in defining her
      role as a woman

8. When you are interviewing clients, it is important to notice and record how they 8.____
say what they say—angrily, nervously, or with "body English" —because these
signs may

A. tell you that the client's words are the opposite of what the client feels and you may need to dig to find out what those feelings are
B. be the prelude to violent behavior which no aide is prepared to handle
C. show that the client does not really deserve serious consideration
D. be important later should you be asked to defend what you did for the client

9. You are recording a visit you have made with a client who was angry and abusive to you during the interview. At one point, you lost your temper and said some things that you immediately regretted. You are embarrassed to record that you lost your temper.
However, it would be desirable to record this MAINLY because
   A. you would feel guilty if you did not record it
   B. your supervisor might hear about it from the client, so it would be better to have it written down from your point of view
   C. your supervisor can use the information to help you to improve your skills
   D. it is agency policy to write down everything

9.____

10. Through one of your clients you learn that a day care program's hours have been extended. You confirm this information with the day care center.
It is then MOST important for you to
   A. make a note of this fact, since it will mean you have to change your schedule in working with the client
   B. add this information to your personal resource file so that you can refer other clients to the day dare program
   C. inform your supervisor of the new information so that it can be added to the central resource file
   D. ignore the information, since your client does not need to have her child in day care for any extra hours

10.____

11. You are sent to a meeting of day-care parents to explain the programs of your agency. One of the parents becomes very angry, saying that welfare departments treat people like animals.
You should remain as calm as possible and say to the parent that
   A. he is right, but you have no control over what your agency does
   B. he is disrupting the meeting and you have come to explain a program, not to listen to complaints
   C. you understand his feelings and that sometimes clients do not get the services they wish as quickly as possible; however, you will do whatever you can to assist him
   D. he should call your supervisor tomorrow and make an appointment to discuss his feelings

11.____

12. Assume that you receive a telephone call from a very angry father. His daughter took money from his wallet, and he wants the caseworker to control the daughter. He yells, screams, and swears at you.
What is the BEST way for you to respond?

12.____

A. Hang up because you are not responsible for his daughter's actions. He shouldn't scream and swear at you.
B. Remember to be courteous and polite at all times, never losing your temper
C. Transfer the call to the supervisor because you are concerned about the father's unreasonableness and do not want the responsibility of dealing with him
D. Tell him that behavior such as he is demonstrating is the reason his daughter steals from him

13. Mrs. D.'s son, aged 12, has been getting into difficulty in the neighborhood. At a community meeting, she asks your help in finding worthwhile activities for him. It is APPROPRIATE for you to respond to her because
    A. you should have knowledge of the social services available in the neighborhood and the activities they offer
    B. you have known Mrs. D. and her family for several years and know how much trouble she has had with her son
    C. it is your job to do what the caseworker assigns to you without question
    D. you are concerned about impressing Mrs. D with your knowledge

14. Several clients live in your neighborhood. They know that you work for the human resources administration. One day one of them tells you that there is a rumor that another client is pregnant and asks if this is true. You know from a past discussion with the caseworker that this client is pregnant.
    The BEST answer for you to give would be to
    A. tell her it is none of her business and if she wants to know, she should ask the caseworker
    B. ask her who told her that this client is pregnant
    C. explain that anything told to the agency is held in confidence and will not be shared with anyone else
    D. tell her you don't know, but will ask when you get back to the office and let her know later

15. The area senior citizens group asks for an agency representative to discuss old-age assistance and new SSI regulations. Your supervisor asks you to attend this meeting; however, you do not wish to go because you really do not feel that you work well with older people. In fact, you don't like them very much.
    What should be your response?
    A. Tell the supervisor that you cannot go because you have an appointment with the doctor that day
    B. Get another worker to go for you and assume his task while he is gone
    C. Explain to your supervisor what problems you have in working with old-age clients
    D. Go, because you should do the tasks that are assigned to you according to your job description

16. At a center where you are distributing literature about agency programs, a citizen comes up to you and begins to complain loudly about agency programs. What should be your response?
    A. Call the police and have the complainer removed from the center
    B. Tell him that you do not make policy; suggest that he go to the office and complain
    C. Remain as calm as possible and ask that he discuss the complaints with you calmly. If necessary, make an appointment with him
    D. Yell at him since this seems to be the way he relates to agency people

17. A community group is having a training program. You are sent to explain agency policy and answer questions.
    Providing this type of contact between the agency and community groups is PROPER because
    A. you like people and are a good public speaker
    B. it is the responsibility of the agency to cooperate with community groups in order to help the public to be well-informed about agency policy
    C. you were once in the same training program and understand the kind of people who are being trained
    D. once in a while everyone should have the opportunity to speak to a community group

18. While you are assisting in the intake area, a young man who is applying is cooperative but begins to ask you personal questions: your age, where you live, whether you have children, and other similar questions.
    You are disturbed by these questions, so you should
    A. tell him that agency policy does not allow you to answer personal questions and send him to another intake worker
    B. tell him it is your responsibility to ask questions, not his
    C. tell your supervisor that you do not want to work in intake because clients can get too nosy and you get nervous
    D. avoid answering personal questions and try to get him to return to the purpose of the interview

19. You are assigned to the reception area for the day. A mother arrives in the office with three small children. In a rage, she says that she does not have enough money to feed the children and demands that you find a home for them.
    The BEST action for you to take should be to
    A. call a security officer and have him remove her and the children from the office
    B. attempt to calm her down by listening to her, attend to the children's needs and call for a supervisor
    C. take the children from her and ask her to leave at once
    D. call the supervisor and security because it is their job to take care of abusive clients

20. Assume that you are interviewing a young unwed mother who has recently arrived in the city from Alabama. She is a likable girl and is very cooperative. However, it is difficult to understand the meaning of her conversation due to her accent and different use of words.
    You would like to establish a good relationship with her, so you should FIRST
    A. suggest that she go to evening school so that she can learn to speak like other people in the city
    B. tell her that you don't understand her sometimes and you would appreciate it if she would explain what she means
    C. take another worker with you on visits to help you in the interview
    D. try to find a worker in the agency who has a similar background and have the case handled by the worker

21. A man being interviewed is entitled to Medicaid, but he refuses to sign up for it because he says he cannot accept any form of welfare.
    Of the following, the BEST course of action for an aide to take FIRST is to
    A. try to discover the reason for his feeling this way
    B. tell him that he should be glad financial help is available
    C. explain that others cannot get help him if he will not help himself
    D. suggest that he speak to someone who is already on Medicaid

22. Of the following, the outcome of an interview by an aide depends MOS heavily on the
    A. personality of the interviewee
    B. personality of the aide
    C. subject matter of the questions asked
    D. interaction between aide and interviewee

23. Some patients being interviewed are PRIMARILY interested in making a favorable impression. The aide should be aware of the fact that such patients are more likely than other patients to
    A. try to anticipate the answers the interviewer is looking for
    B. answer all questions openly and frankly
    C. try to assume the role of interviewer
    D. be anxious to get the interview over as quickly as possible

24. The type of interview which an aide usually conducts is substantially different from most interviewing situations in all of the following aspects EXCEPT the
    A. setting   B. kinds of clients
    C. techniques employed   D. kinds of problems

25. During an interview, an aide uses a "leading question."
    This type of question is so-called because it generally
    A. starts a series of questions about one topic
    B. suggests the answer which the aide wants
    C. forms the basis for a following "trick" question
    D. sets, at the beginning, the tone of the interview

KEY (CORRECT ANSWERS)

1.	C	11.	C
2.	C	12.	B
3.	A	13.	A
4.	B	14.	C
5.	B	15.	C
6.	C	16.	C
7.	A	17.	B
8.	A	18.	D
9.	C	19.	B
10.	C	20.	B

21.	A
22.	D
23.	A
24.	C
25.	B

TEST 2

DIRECTIONS: Each question or incomplete statement is followed by several suggested answers or completions. Select the one that BEST answers the question or completes the statement. *PRINT THE LETTER OF THE CORRECT ANSWER IN THE SPACE AT THE RIGHT.*

1. Miss Lally is an old-age assistance recipient. Her health is not good and it is important that she have three good meals each day. She follows these instructions except on Friday she refuses to eat meat because of her religious beliefs. She will not even substitute fish.
   You are very concerned about this, so you should
   A. tell your supervisor so that she will go to see Miss Lally and make her eat nourishing meals on Friday
   B. call her doctor and tell him so that he will see her and explain to her that fasting is not good for her health
   C. attempt to understand her value system and accept that it is possible that she is acting in good faith with her own values even though they may be harmful to her health
   D. explain to her how important it is that she eat meat each day in order to be in good health and enjoy the remaining years of her life

2. Theodore is a junkie. Every cent he can get his hands on legally or illegally is used to supply his habit. You are angry because the junkie is destroying himself and his family. You feel that the courts should punish him for his illegal acts.
   Of the following, the BEST action for you to take is to
   A. suggest to your supervisor that the income maintenance center reduce the family grant, taking out his portion
   B. help his wife to find another apartment for her and the children away from him
   C. call the local police to find out why they are doing nothing about this man's activities in the community
   D. reconsider your ideas about punishment, remembering that punishment alone will not help the man to change his behavior

3. You are regularly assigned to taking Sarah Jones and her young son to the clinic. She is a very warm, friendly woman and your relationship with her is good. However, she invited you to come for dinner on Sunday and to go to a school play with her. You would like to accept the invitations because you need weekend activities and you like her.
   What should be your PRIMARY consideration in coming to a decision?
   A. You need friends just as she does, so you should accept the invitations
   B. You are a worker and should not be seen with a client in public places
   C. Decide whether accepting the invitations will help to meet agency needs or will hamper the relationship you are expected to establish
   D. Tell her "no" because it is not a good policy to be on such friendly terms with clients

4. Martha's husband has been arrested in a drug raid and she is extremely anxious. Your supervisor asks that you visit her to determine ways in which the agency may help her. You visit and find her weeping; the house and the children have obviously been neglected.
The BEST thing for you to do is to
   A. tell her to stop crying and help her to clean the apartment and the children
   B. remind her that her husband has been warned and now has to pay for not listening
   C. listen to her, allowing her to express her feelings of fear, loss, and grief, and reassure her of your concern
   D. listen to her but caution her that she is neglecting the home and children because of her anxiety and you may have to ask your supervisor to remove the children if she doesn't get any better

4.____

5. Mrs. Dwight's landlord is very slow in making repairs in her apartment. Each time you see her, she complains about this over and over again, calling her landlord names and threatening to report him to the city. She complains to any agency person she meets.
Realizing that these complaints are not getting any action, you should
   A. avoid meeting with her because she is annoying
   B. suggest that she see a doctor because she is irrational and should get some help
   C. ask her what she would like to do about the problem and assist her in carrying out her plans
   D. ask the supervisor to see her because you do not have the skills to help her

5.____

6. In the day-to-day operations of the human resources administration, which of the following would you consider to be the PRIMARY function of the agency?
   A. Getting work done to meet city and federal deadlines
   B. Being sure that all of the clients who come to the agency are seen before closing time
   C. Delivering services to those persons who are eligible for assistance
   D. Making sure everyone gets his check on time

6.____

7. During the course of an interview you find it is necessary to arrange a special appointment for the client to return for a further interview. After checking your calendar, you tell the client the date she is to come back. The client, however, says she cannot see you on that date because she is to attend a rally at a community center in her neighborhood.
Of the following, your BEST action should be to
   A. let her know that any other day is an inconvenience to you and remind her that the appointment is for her benefit
   B. forget about the special appointment and try to get along with the information you have
   C. explain to her the need for the appointment and ask when she can meet with you
   D. tell her that since the community center is not city-operated, she must keep her appointment with you

7.____

8. In working with community groups, it is important that you be able to define what a community is.
Of the following definitions, which is the MOST appropriate?
A community
   A. consists of a group of people living fairly close together in a more or less compact territory, who come together in their chief concerns
   B. is a particular section of a city designated on a census tract
   C. is that portion of a city which constitutes an election district
   D. is a section of a city or town in which a particular ethnic group conducts its social, business, and religious life

8._____

9. The agency has implemented a new policy regarding the intake procedure. You wish to explain and discuss this policy with as many community groups as possible. You make an initial contact by mail.
In order to get your message across well, your letter should be
   A. short and as concise as possible explaining why you want to meet with them, and offer several possible times that you will be available
   B. short, explaining only that it is important that the groups contact you in order to arrange a meeting
   C. drafted by the center's secretary and sent to the usual groups
   D put in the usual announcement form in the center's newsletter

9._____

10. A group of young welfare mothers want to form an organization that will provide babysitting services for mothers of children who are too young to enroll in a day care center.
What should be your answer to them?
   A. Tell them to try to get the center to change its policy to include young children
   B. Arrange the time to meet with them to offer as much advice and support as possible, since most communities do need this service
   C. Suggest that it may be better that they spend their time taking care of their own children
   D. Ask a social worker to survey the community to determine if such a service is really needed at this time

10._____

11. New regulations have removed the disabled, blind, and old-age assistance cases from the public assistance caseload. Assistance in these categories is given directly by the federal government. A former client has not received his check. The chairman of the senior citizens committee calls and angrily demands that your agency do something in this man's behalf.
In response, you should
   A. answer politely, explaining that your agency is not concerned about OAA clients
   B. arrange to meet with him in order to discuss the new policy
   C. refer him to the Social Security office covering the area where the client lives
   D. ask that he call again when he is calmer so that you may discuss this matter with him

11._____

12. A high school student from the community comes to see you about a homework assignment to write a report on your center.
    The BEST way to help him is to
    A. refer him to a social worker who has daily contact with clients in their homes
    B. contact the boy's teacher and find out why you were not warned of his coming
    C. explain your center's program and answer as many of his questions as you can
    D. give him literature about the welfare system in the city and state

13. Assume that the women's group of the Community Baptist Church has invited you to a Sunday afternoon service to celebrate the tenth anniversary of the pastor. The agency's relationship with the women is good in that they often offer their homes as emergency homes for adult clients.
    What should you do about the invitation?
    A. Do not attend but send them a note congratulating the pastor and explaining that agency personnel do not work on Sundays
    B. Ask a social worker who lives close to the church to go
    C. Accept the invitation if at all possible, attend the service and whatever social hour they may have afterwards
    D. Ignore the invitation since this function has little relationship to your job

14. Suppose that a person you are interviewing becomes angry at some of the questions you have asked, calls you meddlesome and nosy, and states that she will not answer those questions.
    Of the following, which is the BEST action for you to take
    A. Explain the reasons the questions are asked and the importance of the answers
    B. Inform the interviewee that you are only doing your job and advise her that she should answer your questions or leave your office
    C. Report to your supervisor what the interviewee called you and refuse to continue the interview
    D. End the interview and tell the interviewee she will not be serviced by your department

15. Suppose that during the course of an interview the interviewee demands in a very rude way that she be permitted to talk to your supervisor or someone in charge.
    Which of the following is probably the BEST way to handle this situation?
    A. Inform your supervisor of the demand and ask her to speak to the interviewee
    B. Pay no attention to the demands of the interviewee and continue the interview
    C. Report to your supervisor and tell her to get another interviewer for this interviewee
    D. Tell her you are the one "in charge" and that she should talk to you

5 (#2)

16. Suppose that a worker asks a client to answer several required but rather personal questions about the family's health history. The client delays and seems embarrassed about giving the answers.
Of the following, the MOST reasonable response to the client is one which
    A. shows an awareness of the client's efforts to hide something
    B. demonstrates the worker's qualifications for asking such questions
    C. allows this client to be excused from answering the questions
    D. convinces the client that his uneasiness in the situation is understood

16.____

17. A representative from a planned parenthood group comes to see you to get information for a community education program.
You should
    A. check out this group to make sure it is not promoting zero population growth for minority groups
    B. develop a good relationship with him so as to provide better service to clients
    C. make sure they will not encourage unnecessary abortions
    D. refuse to see him

17.____

18. A member of a clerical training program is continually late to classes. He explains to you that he has a hard time getting up and asks that you report him on time because he needs to train for a job.
What should your response be?
    A. Tell him that you get there on time and so should he
    B. Tell him that you do not lie for anyone
    C. Explain that it is your duty to keep accurate records and refer him to a counselor
    D. Tell him that you will cooperate with him but he has to try to do better

18.____

19. In a community meeting to explain a new agency policy, you find that the audience has no questions about the policy or your explanations.
What would be the MOST appropriate response to the silence?
    A. Leave right away before they think of questions
    B. Thank the audience for their attention and assure them that you will be available if there are any questions later
    C. Ask several members in the audience if they understand the new policy
    D. Explain that the audience could not possibly understand all of the policy and they must have questions

19.____

20. Assume that you are confronted by an angry member of the public who has not been able to obtain the information he needs from your office. You do not know the answer to his question.
The BEST thing for you to do would be to
    A. tell him to come back another time, after you have looked up the information
    B. check with your supervisor to find the correct answer

20.____

C. tell him to ask in another office, so that you will not lose time looking for the information
D. make up and answer to keep the man satisfied until the right answer is found

KEY (CORRECT ANSWERS)

1.	C	11.	C
2.	D	12.	C
3.	C	13.	C
4.	C	14.	A
5.	C	15.	A
6.	C	16.	D
7.	C	17.	B
8.	A	18.	C
9.	A	19.	B
10.	B	20.	B

EXAMINATION SECTION
TEST 1

DIRECTIONS: Each question or incomplete statement is followed by several suggested answers or completions. Select the one that BEST answers the question or completes the statement. *PRINT THE LETTER OF IN THE CORRECT ANSWER THE SPACE AT THE RIGHT.*

1. Reports show that more men than women are physically handicapped MAINLY because 1.____

   A. women are instinctively more cautious than men
   B. men are more likely to have congenital deformities
   C. women tend to seek surgical remedies because of greater concern over personal appearance
   D. men have lower ability to recover from injury
   E. men are more likely to be exposed to hazardous conditions

2. Of the following, the explanation married women give MOST frequently for seeking employment outside the home is that they wish to 2.____

   A. escape the drudgeries of home life
   B. develop secondary employment skills
   C. maintain an emotionally satisfying career
   D. provide the main support for the family
   E. supplement the family income

3. Of the following home conditions, the one *most likely* to cause emotional disturbances in children is 3.____

   A. increased birthrate following the war
   B. disrupted family relationships
   C. lower family income than that of neighbors
   D. higher family income than that of neighbors
   E. overcrowded living conditions

4. Casual unemployment, as distinguished from other types of unemployment, is traceable MOST readily to 4.____

   A. a decrease in the demand for labor as a result of scientific progress
   B. more or less haphazard changes in the demand for labor in certain industries
   C. periodic changes in the demand for labor in certain industries
   D. disturbances and disruptions in industry resulting from international trade barriers
   E. increased mobility of the population

5. Labor legislation, although primarily intended for the benefit of the employee, MAY aid the employer by 5.____

   A. increasing his control over the immediate labor market
   B. prohibiting government interference with operating policies
   C. protecting him, through equalization of labor costs, from being undercut by other employers
   D. transferring to the general taxpayer the principal costs of industrial hazards of accident and unemployment
   E. increasing the pensions of civil service employees

6. When employment and unemployment figures both decline, the MOST probable conclusion is that

    A. the population has reached a condition of equilibrium
    B. seasonal employment has ended
    C. the labor force has decreased
    D. payments for unemployment insurance have been increased
    E. industrial progress has reduced working hours

7. An individual with an I.Q. of 100 may be said to have demonstrated _____ intelligence.

    A. superior   B. absolute
    C. substandard   D. approximately average
    E. high average

8. While state legislatures differ in many respects, all of them are *most nearly* alike in

    A. provisions for retirement of members
    B. rate of pay
    C. length of legislative sessions
    D. method of selection of their members
    E. length of term of office

9. If a state passed a law in a field under Congressional jurisdiction and if Congress subsequently passed contrary legislation, the state provision would be

    A. regarded as never having existed
    B. valid until the next session of the state legislature, which would be obliged to repeal it
    C. superseded by the federal statute
    D. ratified by Congress
    E. still operative in the state involved

10. Power to pardon offenses committed against the people of the United States is vested in the

    A. Supreme Court of the United States
    B. United States District Courts
    C. Federal Bureau of Investigation
    D. United States Parole Board
    E. President of the United States

11. As distinguished from formal social control of an individual's behavior, an example of informal social control is that exerted by

    A. public opinion   B. religious doctrine
    C. educational institutions   D. statutes
    E. public health measures

12. The PRINCIPAL function of the jury in a jury trial is to decide questions of

    A. equity   B. fact
    C. injunction   D. contract
    E. law

13. Of the following rights of an individual, the one which usually depends on citizenship as distinguished from those given anyone living under the laws of the United States is the right to   13.____

    A. receive public assistance
    B. hold an elective office
    C. petition the government for redress of grievances
    D. receive equal protection of the laws
    E. be accorded a trial by jury

14. If the characteristics of a person were being studied by competent observers, it would be expected that their observations would differ MOST markedly with respect to their evaluation of the person's   14.____

    A. intelligence
    B. nutritional condition
    C. temperamental characteristics
    D. weight
    E. height

15. If there are evidences of dietary deficiency in families where cereals make up a major portion of the diet, the *most likely* reason for this deficiency is that   15.____

    A. cereals cause absorption of excessive quantities of water
    B. persons who concentrate their diet on cereals do not chew their food properly
    C. carbohydrates are deleterious
    D. other essential food elements are omitted
    E. children eat cereals too rapidly

16. Although malnutrition is generally associated with poverty, dietary studies of population groups in the United States reveal that   16.____

    A. malnutrition is most often due to a deficiency of nutrients found chiefly in high-cost foods
    B. there has been overemphasis of the casual relationship between poverty and malnutrition
    C. malnutrition is found among people with sufficient money to be well fed
    D. a majority of the population in all income groups is undernourished
    E. malnutrition is not a factor in the incidence of rickets

17. The organization which has as one of its primary functions the mitigation of suffering caused by famine, fire, floods, and other national calamities is the   17.____

    A. National Safety Council
    B. Salvation Army
    C. Public Administration Service
    D. American National Red Cross
    E. American Legion

18. The MAIN difference between public welfare and private social agencies is that in public agencies,

    A. case records are open to the public
    B. the granting of assistance cannot be sufficiently flexible to meet the varying needs of individual recipients
    C. only financial assistance may be provided
    D. all policies and procedures must be based upon statutory authorizations
    E. economical and efficient administration are stressed because their funds are obtained through public taxation

19. A recipient of relief who is in need of the services of an attorney but is unable to pay the customary fees, should *generally* be referred to the

    A. Small Claims Court
    B. Domestic Relations Court
    C. County Lawyers Association
    D. City Law Department
    E. Legal Aid Society

20. An injured workman should file his claim for workmen's compensation with the

    A. State Labor Relations Board
    B. Division of Placement and Unemployment Insurance
    C. State Industrial Commission
    D. Workmen's Compensation Board
    E. State Insurance Board

21. The type of insurance found MOST frequently among families such as those assisted by the Department of Social Services is

    A. accident   B. straight life
    C. endowment   D. industrial
    E. personal liability

22. Of the following items in the standard budget of the Department of Social Services, the one for which actual expenditures would be MOST constant throughout the year is

    A. fuel   B. housing
    C. medical care   D. clothing
    E. household replacements

23. The MOST frequent cause of "broken homes" is attributed to the

    A. temperamental incompatibilities of parents and in-laws
    B. extension of the system of children's courts
    C. psychopathic irresponsibility of the parents
    D. institutionalization of one of the spouses
    E. death of one or both spouses

24. In rearing children, the problems of the widower are usually greater than those of the widow, largely because of the

   A. tendency of widowers to impose excessively rigid moral standards
   B. increased economic hardship
   C. added difficulty of maintaining a desirable home
   D. possibility that a stepmother will be added to the household
   E. prevalent masculine prejudice against pursuits which are inherently feminine

25. Foster-home placement of children is often advocated in preference to institutionalization *primarily* because

   A. the law does not provide for local supervision of children's institutions
   B. institutions furnish a more expensive type of care
   C. the number of institutions is insufficient compared to the number of children needing care
   D. children are not well treated in institutions
   E. foster homes provide a more normal environment for children

KEY (CORRECT ANSWERS)

1.	E	11.	A
2.	E	12.	B
3.	B	13.	B
4.	B	14.	C
5.	C	15.	D
6.	C	16.	C
7.	D	17.	D
8.	D	18.	D
9.	C	19.	E
10.	E	20.	D

21.	D
22.	B
23.	E
24.	C
25.	E

TEST 2

DIRECTIONS: Each question or incomplete statement is followed by several suggested answers or completions. Select the one that BEST answers the question or completes the statement. *PRINT THE LETTER OF THE CORRECT ANSWER IN THE SPACE AT THE RIGHT.*

1. Of the following, the category MOST likely to yield the greatest reduction in cost to the taxpayer under improved employment conditions is 1.____

    A. home relief, including aid to the homeless
    B. aid to the blind
    C. aid to dependent children
    D. old-age assistance

2. One of the MOST common characteristics of the chronic alcoholic is 2.____

    A. low intelligence level
    B. wanderlust
    C. psychosis
    D. egocentricity

3. Of the following factors leading toward the cure of the alcoholic, the MOST important is thought to be 3.____

    A. removal of all alcohol from the immediate environment
    B. development of a sense of personal adequacy
    C. social disapproval of drinking
    D. segregation from former companions

4. The Federal Housing Administration is the agency which 4.____

    A. insures mortgages made by lending institutions for new construction or remodeling of old construction
    B. provides federal aid for state and local government for slum clearance and housing for very low income families
    C. subsidizes the building industry through direct grants
    D. provides for the construction of low-cost housing projects owned and operated by the federal government

5. In comparing the advantages of foster home over institutional placement, it is generally agreed that institutional care is LEAST advisable for children 5.____

    A. who cannot sustain the intimacy of foster family living because of their experiences with their own parents
    B. who are socially well-adjusted or have had considerable experience in living with a family
    C. who have need for special facilities for observation, diagnosis, and treatment
    D. whose natural parents find it difficult to accept the idea of foster home placement because of its close resemblance to adoption

6. The school can play a vital part in detecting the child who displays overt symptomatic behavior indicative of social maladjustment CHIEFLY because the teacher has the opportunity to

   A. assume a pseudo-parental role in regard to discipline and punishment, thereby limiting the extent of the maladjusted child's anti-social behavior
   B. observe how the child relates to the group and what reactions are stimulated in him by his peer relationships
   C. determine whether the adjustment difficulties displayed by the child were brought on by the teacher herself or by the other students
   D. help the child's parents to resolve the difficulties in adjustment which are indicated by the child's reactions to the social pressures exerted by his peers

7. In treating juvenile delinquents, it has been found that there are some who make better social adjustment through group treatment than through an individual casework approach.
   In selecting delinquent boys for group treatment, the one of the following which is the MOST important consideration is that

   A. the boys to be treated in one group be friends or from the same community
   B. only boys who consent to group treatment be included in the group
   C. the ages of the boys included in the group vary as much as possible
   D. only boys who have not reacted to an individual casework approach be included in the group

8. Multi-problem families are generally characterized by various functional indicators.
   Of the following, the family which is *most likely* to be a multi-problem family is one which has

   A. unemployed adult family members
   B. parents with diagnosed character disorders
   C. children and parents with a series of difficulties in the community
   D. poor housekeeping standards

9. Multi-problem families generally have a complex history of intervention by a variety of social agencies.
   Of the following phases involved in planning for their treatment, the one which is MOST important to consider FIRST is the

   A. joint decision to limit any help to be given
   B. analysis of facts and definition of the problems involved
   C. determination of treatment priorities
   D. study of available community resources

10. The development of good public relations in the area for which the supervisor is responsible should be considered by the supervisor as

    A. not his responsibility as he is primarily responsible for his workers' services
    B. dependent upon him as he is in the best position to interpret the department to the community
    C. not important to the adequate functioning of the department
    D. a part of his method of carrying out his job responsibility as what his workers do affects the community

11. Of the following, the LEAST accurate statement concerning the relationship of public and private social agencies is that

    A. both have an important and necessary function to perform
    B. they are not to be considered as competing or rival agencies
    C. they are cooperating agencies
    D. their work is based on fundamentally different social work concepts

12. Of the following, the LEAST accurate statement concerning the worker-client relationship is that the worker should have the ability to

    A. express warmth of feeling in appropriate ways as a basis for a professional relationship which creates confidence
    B. feel appropriately in the relationship without losing the ability to see the situation in the perspective necessary to help the people immersed in it
    C. identify himself with the client so that the worker's personality does not influence the client
    D. use keen observation and perceive what is significant with a new range of appreciation of the meaning of the situation to the client

13. Of the following, the MOST fundamental psychological concept underlying case work in the public assistance field is that

    A. eligibility for public assistance should be reviewed from time to time
    B. workers should be aware of the prevalence of psychological disabilities among members of families on public assistance
    C. workers should realize the necessity of carrying out the policies laid down by the state office in order that state aid may be received
    D. in the process of receiving assistance, recipients should not be deprived of their normal status of self-direction

14. Of the following, the MOST comprehensive as well as the MOST accurate statement concerning the professional attitude of the social worker is that he should

    A. have a real concern for, and an intelligent interest in, the welfare of the client
    B. recognize that the client's feelings rather than the realities of his needs are of major importance to the client
    C. put at the client's service the worker's knowledge and sincere interest in him
    D. use his insight and understanding to make sound decisions about the client

15. The one of the following reasons for refusing a job which is LEAST acceptable, from the viewpoint of maintaining a client's continued rights to unemployment insurance benefits, is that

    A. acceptance of the job would interfere with the client's joining or retaining membership in a labor union
    B. there is a strike, lockout, or other industrial controversy in the establishment where employment is offered
    C. the distance from the place of employment to his home is greater than seems justified to the client
    D. the wages offered are lower than the prevailing wages in that locality

16. Experience pragmatically suggests that dislocation from cultural roots and customs makes for tension, insecurity, and anxiety. This holds for the child as well as the adolescent, for the new immigrant as well as the second-generation citizen.
    Of the following, the MOST important implication of the above statement for a social worker in any setting is that

    A. anxiety, distress, and incapacity are always personal and can be understood best only through an understanding of the child's present cultural environment
    B. in order to resolve the conflicts caused by the displacement of a child from a home with one cultural background to one with another, it is essential that the child fully replace his old culture with the new one
    C. no treatment goal can be envisaged for a dislocated child which does not involve a value judgment which is itself culturally determined
    D. anxiety and distress result from a child's reaction to culturally oriented treatment goals

17. Accepting the fact that mentally gifted children represent superior heredity, the United States faces an important eugenic problem CHIEFLY because

    A. unless these mentally gifted children mature and reproduce more rapidly than the less intelligent children, the nation is heading for a lowering of the average intelligence of its people
    B. although the mentally gifted child always excels scholastically, he generally has less physical stamina than the normal child and tends to lower the nation's population physically
    C. the mentally subnormal are increasing more rapidly than the mentally gifted in America, thus affecting the overall level of achievement of the gifted child
    D. unless the mental level of the general population is raised to that of the gifted child, the mentally gifted will eventually usurp the reigns of government and dominate the mentally weaker

18. The form of psychiatric treatment which requires the LEAST amount of participation on the part of the patient is

    A. psychoanalysis
    B. psychotherapy
    C. shock therapy
    D. non-directive therapy

19. Tests administered by psychologists for the PRIMARY purpose of measuring intelligence are known as _____ tests.

    A. projective
    B. validating
    C. psychometric
    D. apperception

20. In recent years, there have been some significant changes in the treatment of patients in state psychiatric hospitals. These changes are PRIMARILY caused by the use of

    A. electric shock therapy
    B. tranquilizing drugs
    C. steroids
    D. the open-ward policy

21. The psychological test which makes use of a set of twenty pictures, each depicting a dramatic scene, is known as the

    A. Goodenough Test
    B. Thematic Apperception Test
    C. Minnesota Multiphasic Personality Inventory
    D. Healy Picture Completion Test

22. One of the MOST effective ways in which experimental psychologists have been able to study the effects on personality of heredity and environment has been through the study of

    A. primitive cultures
    B. identical twins
    C. mental defectives
    D. newborn infants

23. In hospitals with psychiatric divisions, the psychiatric function is PREDOMINANTLY that of

    A. the training of personnel in all psychiatric disciplines
    B. protection of the community against potentially dangerous psychiatric patients
    C. research and study of psychiatric patients so that new knowledge and information can be made generally available
    D. short-term hospitalization designed to determine diagnosis and recommendations for treatment

24. Predictions of human behavior on the basis of past behavior frequently are INACCURATE because

    A. basic patterns of human behavior are in a continual state of flux
    B. human behavior is not susceptible to explanation of a scientific nature
    C. the underlying psychological mechanisms of behavior are not completely understood
    D. quantitative techniques for the measurement of stimuli and responses are unavailable

25. Socio-cultural factors are being re-evaluated in casework practice as they influence both the worker and the client in their participation in the casework process.
    Of the following factors, the one which is currently being studied MOST widely is the

    A. social class of worker and client and its significance in casework
    B. difference in native intelligence which can be ascribed to racial origin of an individual
    C. cultural values affecting the areas in which an individual functions
    D. necessity in casework treatment of the client's membership in an organized religious group

25.____

KEY (CORRECT ANSWERS)

1. A
2. D
3. B
4. A
5. B

6. B
7. B
8. C
9. B
10. D

11. D
12. C
13. D
14. C
15. C

16. C
17. A
18. C
19. C
20. B

21. B
22. B
23. D
24. C
25. C

INTERVIEWING
EXAMINATION SECTION
TEST 1

DIRECTIONS: Each question or incomplete statement is followed by several suggested answers or completions. Select the one that BEST answers the question or completes the statement. *PRINT THE LETTER OF THE CORRECT ANSWER IN THE SPACE AT THE RIGHT.*

1. You are conducting an interview with a client who has been having some difficulties with one of her fellow-workers. The client walks on crutches. You tell the client that she probably finds it difficult to get along with her fellow-workers because of this handicap.
To make such a statement would, *generally*, be

    A. *proper;* people are often prejudiced against persons with physical deformities
    B. *proper;* statements such as this indicate to the client that you are sympathetic toward her
    C. *improper;* this approach would not help the client solve her problem
    D. *improper;* you should have discussed this handicap in relation to the client's continued ability to continue in her job

2. The information which the interviewer plans to secure from an individual with whom he talks is determined MAINLY by the

    A. purpose of the interview and the functions of the agency
    B. state assistance laws and the desires of the individual
    C. privacy they have while talking and the willingness of the individual to give information
    D. emotional feelings of the individual seeking help and the interviewer's reactions to these feelings

3. *Generally,* the MOST effective of the following ways of dealing with a person being interviewed who frequently digresses from the subject under discussion or starts to ramble, is for the interviewer to

    A. tell the person that he, the interviewer, will have to terminate the interview unless the former sticks to the point
    B. increase the tempo of the interview
    C. demonstrate that he is a good listener and allow the person to continue in his own way
    D. inject questions which relate to the purpose of the interview

4. "Being a good listener" is an interviewing technique which, if applied properly, is *desirable* MOSTLY because it

    A. catches the client more easily in misrepresentations and lies
    B. conserves the energies of the interviewer
    C. encourages the client to talk about his personal affairs without restraint
    D. encourages the giving of information which is generally more reliable and complete

5. When questioning applicants for eligibility, it would be BEST to ask questions that are

A. *direct,* so that the applicant will realize that the interviewer knows what he is doing
B. *direct,* so that the information received will be as pertinent as possible
C. *indirect,* so that the applicant will not realize the purpose of the interview
D. *indirect,* so that you can trap the applicant into making admissions that he would not otherwise make

6. The CHIEF reason for conducting an interview with a new applicant in complete privacy is that the

   A. interviewer will be better able to record the facts without any other worker reading his case notes
   B. applicant will be impressed by the business-like atmosphere of the agency
   C. interviewer will be able to devote more time to questioning the applicant without interruption
   D. applicant will be more likely to speak frankly

7. When conducting an interview with a client who is upset because of an increase in rent, it would be BEST for the interviewer to

   A. agree with the client that the agency was wrong in raising his rent, as a basis for further discussion
   B. tell the client that unless he calms down the interview will be ended
   C. prevent the client from becoming emotional
   D. tell the client the reasons for the increase

8. At an interview to determine whether an applicant is eligible, the applicant gives information different from that which he submitted on his application.
The MOST advisable action to take is to

   A. cross out the old information, enter the new information, and initial the entry
   B. re-enter the old information on the application form and initial the entry
   C. give the applicant another application form, have him fill it out correctly, and resume the interview
   D. give the applicant another application form to fill out, and set a later date for another interview

9. After you have secured, in an interview, all the necessary information from an applicant, he shows no intention of leaving, but starts to tell you a long personal story.
Of the following, the MOST advisable action for you to take is to

   A. explain to the applicant why personal stories are out of place in a business office
   B. listen carefully to the story for whatever relevant information it may contain
   C. interrupt him tactfully, thank him for the information he has already given, and terminate the interview
   D. inform your supervisor that the time required for this interview will prevent you from completing the interviews scheduled for the day

10. In interviewing, the practice of anticipating an applicant's answers to questions is, *generally,*

    A. *desirable* because it is effective and economical when it is necessary to interview large numbers of applicants
    B. *desirable* because many applicants have language difficulties

C. *undesirable* because it is the inalienable right of every person to answer as he sees fit
D. *undesirable* because applicants may tend to agree with the answer proposed by the interviewer even when the answer is not entirely correct

11. A follow-up interview was arranged for an applicant in order that he might furnish certain requested evidence. At this follow-up interview, the applicant still fails to furnish the necessary evidence.
It would be MOST advisable for you to

    A. advise the applicant that he is now considered ineligible
    B. ask the applicant how soon he can get the necessary evidence and set a date for another interview
    C. question the applicant carefully and thoroughly to determine if he has misrepresented or falsified any information
    D. set a date for another interview and tell the applicant to get the necessary evidence by that time

12. When an initial interview is being conducted, one way of starting is to explain the purpose of the interview to the applicant.
The practice of starting the interview with such an explanation is, *generally,*

    A. *desirable* because the applicant can then understand why the interview is necessary and what will be accomplished by it
    B. *desirable* because it creates the rapport which is necessary to successful interviewing
    C. *undesirable* because time will be saved by starting off directly with the questions which must be asked
    D. *undesirable* because the interviewer should have the choice of starting an interview in any manner he prefers

13. Empathy can be defined as the ability of one individual to respond sensitively and imaginatively to another's feelings.
For an interviewer to be empathic during an interview is *usually*

    A. *undesirable*, mainly because an interviewer should never be influenced by the feelings of the one being interviewed
    B. *desirable*, mainly because an interview will not be productive unless the interviewer takes the side of the person interviewed
    C. *undesirable*, mainly because empathy usually leads an interviewer to be biased in favor of the person being interviewed
    D. *desirable*, mainly because this ability allows the interviewer to direct his questions more effectively to the person interviewed

14. Assume that you must interview several people who know each other.
To gather them all in one group and question them TOGETHER, is, *generally,*

    A. *good practice,* since any inaccurate information offered by one person would be corrected by others in the group
    B. *poor practice,* since people in a group rarely pay adequate attention to questions
    C. *good practice,* since the interviewer will save much time and effort in this way
    D. *poor practice,* since the presence of several people can inhibit an individual from speaking

15. An effective interviewer should know that the one of the following reasons which LEAST describes why there is a wide range of individual behavior in human relations is that

    A. socio-economic status influences human behavior
    B. physical characteristics do not influence human behavior
    C. education influences human behavior
    D. childhood experience influences human behavior

16. An interviewer encounters an uncooperative interviewee. Of the following, the FIRST thing the interviewer should do in such a situation is to

    A. try various appeals to win the interviewee over to a cooperative attitude
    B. try to ascertain the reason for non-cooperation
    C. promise the interviewee that all data will be kept confidential
    D. alter his interviewing technique with the uncooperative interviewee

17. You discover that an interviewee who was requested to bring with him specific documents for his initial employment interview has forgotten the documents.
    Of the following, the BEST course of action to take is to

    A. give the person a reasonable amount of time to furnish the documents
    B. tell the person you will let him know how much additional time he has
    C. mark the person disqualified for employment; he has failed to provide reasonably requested data on time
    D. mark the person provisionally qualified for employment; upon receipt of the documents he will be permanently qualified

18. In checking interviewees' work experience, you realize that the person whom you are to interview is only marginally fluent in English and has, therefore, requested permission to bring a translator with him.
    Of the following, the BEST course of action is to inform the interviewee that

    A. outside translators may not be used
    B. only city translators may be used
    C. state law requires fluency in English of all civil servants
    D. he may be assisted in the interview by his translator

19. Assume that, during the course of an interview, you are verbally attacked by the person being interviewed.
    Of the following, it would be MOST advisable to

    A. answer back in a matter-of-fact manner
    B. ask the person to apologize and discontinue the interview
    C. ignore the attack but adjourn the interview to another day
    D. use restraint and continue the interview

20. Assume that you find that the person you are interviewing has difficulty finishing his sentences and seems to be groping for words.
    In such a case, the BEST approach for you to take is to

    A. say what you think the person has in mind
    B. proceed patiently without calling attention to the problem
    C. ask the person why he finds it difficult to finish his sentences
    D. interrupt the interview until the person feels more relaxed

21. The one of the following which BEST describes the effect of the *sympathetic approach* in interviewing on the interviewee is that it will

    A. have no discernible effect on the interviewee
    B. calm the interviewee
    C. lead the interviewee to underemphasize his problems
    D. mislead the interviewee

22. The one of the following characteristics which is a PRIMARY requisite for a successful interview is

    A. total *curiosity*
    B. total *sympathy*
    C. complete *attention*
    D. complete *dedication*

23. Assume that you have been assigned to conduct a follow-up interview with a primary witness.
    The one of the following which is MOST important in arranging such an interview is to

    A. keep the witness cooperative
    B. conduct the matter in secret
    C. allow the witness to determine where and when the interview takes place
    D. conduct the interview as soon as possible to insure a strong case

24. By examining a candidate's employment record, an interviewer can determine many things about the candidate. Of the following, the one which is LEAST apparent from an employment record is the candidate's

    A. character
    B. willingness to work
    C. capacity to get along with co-workers
    D. potential for advancing in civil service

25. Assume that you are conducting an interview in which the person being interviewed is using the interview as a forum for venting his anti-civil service feelings.
    Of the following, the FIRST thing that you should do is to

    A. agree with the person; perhaps that will shorten the outburst
    B. respectfully disagree with the person; the decorum of the interview has already been disrupted
    C. courteously and objectively direct the interview to the relevant issue
    D. reschedule the interview to another mutually agreeable time

KEY (CORRECT ANSWERS)

1. C
2. A
3. D
4. D
5. B

6. D
7. D
8. A
9. C
10. D

11. B
12. A
13. D
14. D
15. B

16. B
17. A
18. D
19. D
20. B

21. C
22. C
23. A
24. D
25. C

TEST 2

DIRECTIONS: Each question or incomplete statement is followed by several suggested answers or completions. Select the one that BEST answers the question or completes the statement. *PRINT THE LETTER OF THE CORRECT ANSWER IN THE SPACE AT THE RIGHT.*

1. The pattern of an interview is LARGELY set by the   1.____

   A. person being interviewed
   B. person conducting the interview
   C. nature of the interview
   D. policy of the agency employing the interviewer

2. Assume that a person being interviewed, who had been talking freely, suddenly tries to change the subject.   2.____
   To a trained interviewer, this behavior would mean that the person *probably*

   A. knew very little about the subject
   B. realized that he was telling too much
   C. decided that his privacy was being violated
   D. realized that he was becoming confused

3. Assume that you receive a telephone call from an unknown individual requesting information about a person you are currently interviewing.   3.____
   In such a situation, the BEST course of action for you to take is to

   A. give him the information over the telephone
   B. tell him to write to your department for the information
   C. send him the information, retaining a copy for your files
   D. tell him to call back, giving you additional time to check into the matter

4. In an interview, assuming that the interviewer was using a *non-directive approach* in this interview, of the following, the interviewer's most effective response would be: 4.____

   A. "You know, you are building a bad record of tardiness."
   B. "Can you tell me more about this situation?"
   C. "What kind of person is your superior?"
   D. "Do you think you are acting fairly towards the agency by being late so often?"

5. In an interview, assuming that the interviewer was using a *directed approach* in this interview, of the following, the interviewer's response should be: 5.____

   A. "That doesn't seem like much of an excuse to me."
   B. "What do you mean by saying that you've lost interest?"
   C. "What problems are there with the supervision you are getting?"
   D. "How do you think your tardiness looks in your personnel record?"

Questions 6-8.

DIRECTIONS: Answer Questions 6 through 8 only on the basis of information given in the passage below.

A personnel interviewer, selecting job applicants, may find that he reacts badly to some people even on first contact. This reaction cannot usually be explained by things that the interviewee has done or said. Most of us have had the experience of liking or disliking, of feeling comfortable or uncomfortable with people on first acquaintance, long before we have had a chance to make a conscious, rational decision about them. Often, too, our liking or disliking is transmitted to the other person by subtle processes such as gestures, posture, voice intonations, or choice of words. The point to be kept in mind in this: the relations between people are complex and occur at several levels, from the conscious to the unconscious. This is true whether the relationship is brief or long, formal or informal.

Some of the major dynamics of personality which operate on the unconscious level are projection, sublimation, rationalization, and repression. Encountering these for the first time, one is apt to think of them as representing pathological states. In the extreme, they undoubtedly are, but they exist so universally that we must consider them also to be parts of normal personality.

Without necessarily subscribing to any of the numerous theories of personality, it is possible to describe personality in terms of certain important aspects or elements. We are all aware of ourselves as thinking organisms.

This aspect of personality, the conscious part, is important for understanding human behavior, but it is not enough. Many find it hard to accept the notion that each person also has an unconscious. The existence of the unconscious is no longer a matter of debate. It is not possible to estimate at all precisely what proportion of our total psychological life is conscious, what proportion unconscious. Everyone who has studied the problem, however, agrees that consciousness is the smaller part of personality. Most of what we are and do is a result of unconscious processes. To ignore this is to risk mistakes.

6. The passage above suggests that an interviewer can be MOST effective if he

   A. learns how to determine other peoples' unconscious motivations
   B. learns how to repress his own unconsciously motivated mannerisms and behavior
   C. can keep others from feeling that he either likes or dislikes them
   D. gains an understanding of how the unconscious operates in himself and in others

7. It may be inferred from the passage above that the "subtle processes, such as gestures, posture, voice intonation, or choice of words," referred to in the first paragraph, are, *usually,*

   A. in the complete control of an expert interviewer
   B. the determining factors in the friendships a person establishes
   C. controlled by a person's unconscious
   D. not capable of being consciously controlled

8. The passage above implies that various different personality theories are, *usually,*

   A. so numerous and different as to be valueless to an interviewer
   B. in basic agreement about the importance of the unconscious
   C. understood by the interviewer who strives to be effective
   D. in agreement that personality factors such as projection and repression are pathological

Questions 9-10.

DIRECTIONS: Answer Questions 9 and 10 ONLY on the basis of information given in the passage below.

Since we generally assure informants that what they say is confidential, we are not free to tell one informant what the other has told us. Even if the informant says, "I don't care who knows it; tell anybody you want to," we find it wise to treat the interview as confidential. An interviewer who relates to some informants what other informants have told him is likely to stir up anxiety and suspicion. Of course, the interviewer may be able to tell an informant what he has heard without revealing the source of his information. This may be perfectly appropriate where a story has wide currency so that an informant cannot infer the source of the information. But if an event is not widely known, the mere mention of it may reveal to one informant what another informant has said about the situation. How can the data be cross-checked in these circumstances?

9. The passage above implies that the anxiety and suspicion an interviewer may arouse by telling what has been learned in other interviews is due to the

    A. lack of trust the person interviewed may have in the interviewer's honesty
    B. troublesome nature of the material which the interviewer has learned in other interviews
    C. fact that the person interviewed may not believe that permission was given to repeat the information
    D. fear of the person interviewed that what he is telling the interviewer will be repeated

9._____

10. The paragraph above is *most likely* part of a longer passage dealing with

    A. ways to verify data gathered in interviews
    B. the various anxieties a person being interviewed may feel
    C. the notion that people sometimes say things they do not mean
    D. ways an interviewer can avoid seeming suspicious

10._____

Questions 11-12.

DIRECTIONS: Answer Questions 11 and 12 ONLY on the basis of information given below.

The ability to interview rests not only on any single trait, but on a vast complex of them. Habits, skills, techniques, and attitudes are all involved. Competence in interviewing is acquired only after careful and diligent study, prolonged practice (preferably under supervision), and a good bit of trial and error; for interviewing is not an exact science, it is an art. Like many other arts, however, it can and must draw on science in several of its aspects.

There is always a place for individual initiative, for imaginative innovations, and for new combinations of old approaches. The skilled interviewer cannot be bound by a set of rules. Likewise, there is not a set of rules which can guarantee to the novice that his interviewing will be successful. There are, however, some accepted, general guide-posts which may help the beginner to avoid mistakes, learn how to conserve his efforts, and establish effective working relationships with interviewees; to accomplish, in short, what he set out to do.

11. According to the passage above, rules and standard techniques for interviewing are

11._____

A. helpful for the beginner, but useless for the experienced, innovative interviewer
B. destructive of the innovation and initiative needed for a good interviewer
C. useful for even the experienced interviewer, who may, however, sometimes go beyond them
D. the means by which nearly anybody can become an effective interviewer

12. According to the passage above, the one of the following which is a prerequisite to competent interviewing is   12.____

   A. avoiding mistakes
   B. study and practice
   C. imaginative innovation
   D. natural aptitude

Questions 13-16.

DIRECTIONS: Answer Questions 13 through 16 SOLELY on the basis of information given in the following paragraph.

The question of what material is relevant is not as simple as it might seem. Frequently material which seems irrelevant to the inexperienced has, because of the common tendency to disguise and distort and misplace one's feelings, considerable significance. It may be necessary to let the client "ramble on" for a while in order to clear the decks, as it were, so that he may get down to things that really are on his mind. On the other hand, with an already disturbed person, it may be important for the interviewer to know when to discourage further elaboration of upsetting material. This is especially the case where the worker would be unable to do anything about it. An inexperienced interviewer might, for instance, be intrigued with the bizarre elaboration of material that the psychotic produces, but further elaboration of this might encourage the client in his instability. A too random discussion may indicate that the interviewee is not certain in what areas the interviewer is prepared to help him, and he may be seeking some direction. Or again, satisfying though it may be for the interviewer to have the interviewee tell him intimate details, such revelations sometimes need to be checked or encouraged only in small doses. An interviewee who has "talked too much" often reveals subsequent anxiety. This is illustrated by the fact that? frequently after a "confessional" interview ,the interviewee surprises the interviewer by being withdrawn, inarticulate, or hostile, or by breaking the next appointment.

13. Sometimes a client may reveal certain personal information to an interviewer and subsequently, may feel anxious about this revelation.   13.____
   If, during an interview, a client begins to discuss very personal matters, it would be BEST to

   A. tell the client, in no uncertain terms, that you're not interested in personal details
   B. ignore the client at this point
   C. encourage the client to elaborate further on the details
   D. inform the client that the information seems to be very personal

14. Clients with severe psychological disturbances pose an especially difficult problem for the inexperienced interviewer.
The difficulty lies in the possibility of the client's

    A. becoming physically violent and harming the interviewer
    B. "rambling on" for a while
    C. revealing irrelevant details which may be followed by cancelled appointments
    D. reverting to an unstable state as a result of interview material

14.____

15. An interviewer should be constantly alert to the possibility of obtaining clues from the client as to problem areas.
According to the above passage, a client who discusses topics at random may be

    A. unsure of what problems the interviewer can provide help
    B. reluctant to discuss intimate details
    C. trying to impress the interviewer with his knowledge
    D. deciding what relevant material to elaborate on

15.____

16. The evaluation of a client's responses may reveal substantial information that may aid the interviewer in assessing the problem areas that are of concern to the client. Responses that seemed irrelevant at the time of the interview may be of significance because

    A. considerable significance is attached to all irrelevant material
    B. emotional feelings are frequently masked
    C. an initial "rambling on" is often a prelude to what -is actually bothering the client
    D. disturbed clients often reveal subsequent anxiety

16.____

Questions 17-19.

DIRECTIONS: Answer Questions 17 through 19 SOLELY on the basis of the following paragraph.

The physical setting of the interview may determine its entire potentiality. Some degree of privacy and a comfortable relaxed atmosphere are important. The interviewee is not encouraged to give much more than his name and address if the interviewer seems busy with other things, if people are rushing about, if there are distracting noises. He has a right to feel that, whether the interview lasts five minutes or an hour, he has, for that time, the undivided attention of the interviewer. Interruptions, telephone calls, and so on, should be reduced to a minimum. If the interviewee has waited in a crowded room for what seems to him an interminably long period, he is naturally in no mood to sit down and discuss what is on his mind. Indeed, by that time the primary thing on his mind may be his irritation at being kept waiting, and he frequently feels it would be impolite to express this. If a wait or interruptions have been unavoidable, it is always helpful to give the client some recognition that these are disturbing and that he can naturally understand that they make it more difficult for him to proceed. At the same time if he protests that they have not troubled him, the interviewer can best accept his statements at their face value, as further insistence that they must have been disturbing may be interpreted by him as accusing, and he may conclude that the interviewer has been personally hurt by his irritation.

6 (#2)

17. Distraction during an interview may tend to limit the client's responses.
In a case where an interruption has occurred, it would be BEST for the interviewer to

   A. terminate this interview and have it rescheduled for another time period
   B. ignore the interruption since it is not continuous
   C. express his understanding that the distraction can cause the client to feel disturbed
   D. accept the client's protests that he has been troubled by the interruption

18. To maximize the rapport that can be established with the client, an appropriate physical setting is necessary. At the very least, some privacy would be necessary.
In addition, the interviewer should

   A. always appear to be busy in order to impress the client
   B. focus his attention only on the client
   C. accept all the client's statements as being valid
   D. stress the importance of the interview to the client

19. Clients who have been waiting quite some time for their interview may, justifiably, become upset. However, a client *may initially* attempt to mask these feelings because he may

   A. personally hurt the interviewer
   B. want to be civil
   C. feel that the wait was unavoidable
   D. fear the consequences of his statement

20. You have been assigned to interview W, a witness, concerning a minor automobile accident. Although you have made no breach of the basic rules of contact and approach, you, nevertheless, recognize that you and W have a personality clash and that a natural animosity has resulted.
Of the following, you MOST appropriately should

   A. discuss the personality problem with W and attempt to resolve the difference
   B. stop the interview on some pretext and leave in a calm and pleasant manner, allowing an associate to continue the interview
   C. ignore the personality problem and continue as though nothing had happened
   D. change the subject matter being discussed since the facts sought may be the source of the animosity

21. Assume that you desire to interview W, a reluctant witness to an event that took place several weeks previously. Assume further that the interview can take place at a location to be designated by the interviewer.
Of the following, the place of interview should *preferably* be the

   A. office of the interviewer
   B. home of W
   C. office of W
   D. scene where the event took place

22. Assume that you are interviewing W, a witness. During the interview it becomes apparent that W's statements are inaccurate and at variance with the facts previously established.
In these circumstances, it would be BEST for you to

   A. tell W that his statements are inaccurate and point out how they conflict with previously established facts

B. reword your questions and ask additional questions about the facts being discussed
C. warn W that he may be required to testify under oath at a later date
D. ignore W's statements if you have other information that support the facts

23. Assume that W, a witness being interviewed by you, shows a tendency to ramble. His answers to your questions are lengthy and not responsive.
In this situation, the BEST action for you to take is to

   A. permit W to continue because at some point he will tell you the information sought
   B. tell W that he is rambling and unresponsive and that more will be accomplished if he is brief and to the point
   C. control the interview so that complete and accurate information is obtained
   D. patiently listen to W since rambling is W's style and it cannot be changed

24. Assume that you are interviewing a client. Of the following, the BEST procedure for you to follow in regard to the use of your notebook is to

   A. take out your notebook at the start of the interview and immediately begin taking notes
   B. memorize the important facts related during the interview and enter them after the interview has been completed
   C. advise the client that all his answers are being taken down to insure that he will tell the truth
   D. establish rapport with the client and ask permission to jot down various data in your notebook

25. In order to conduct an effective interview, an interviewer's attention must continuously be directed in two ways, toward himself as well as toward the interviewee. Of the following, the PRIMARY danger in this division of attention is that the

   A. interviewer's behavior may become less natural and thus alienate the interviewee
   B. interviewee's span of attention will be shortened
   C. interviewer's response may be interpreted by the interviewee as being antagonistic
   D. interviewee's more or less concealed prejudices will come to the surface

KEY (CORRECT ANSWERS)

1. B
2. B
3. B
4. B
5. C

6. D
7. C
8. B
9. D
10. A

11. C
12. B
13. D
14. D
15. A

16. B
17. C
18. B
19. B
20. B

21. A
22. B
23. C
24. D
25. A

READING COMPREHENSION
UNDERSTANDING AND INTERPRETING WRITTEN MATERIAL
EXAMINATION SECTION
TEST 1

DIRECTIONS: Each question or incomplete statement is followed by several suggested answers or completions. Select the one that BEST answers the question or completes the statement. *PRINT THE LETTER OF THE CORRECT ANSWER IN THE SPACE AT THE RIGHT.*

Questions 1-8.

DIRECTIONS: Questions 1 through 8 are to be answered on the basis of the following passage.

    The child lives in a context which is itself neither simple nor unitary and which continuously affects his behavior and development. Patterns of stimulation come to him out of this context. In turn, by virtue of his own make-up, he selects from that context. At all times, there is a reciprocal relation between the human organism and his biosocial context. Because the child is limited in time, behavior becomes structured, and patterns develop both in the stimulus field and in his own response system. Some stimulus patterns become significant because they modify the developmental stream by affecting practice or social relations with others. Others remain insignificant because they do not affect this web of relations. Why one pattern is significant and another is not is a crucial problem for child psychology.

1. The author states that
    A. environmental forces have an important effect in determining both the child's actions and his course of growth
    B. environmental and hereditary forces play an equal part in determining both the child's actions and his course of growth
    C. even the environmental forces which are not consciously important to the child can affect both learning and personality
    D. the child's personality is shaped more by the total pattern of pressures in the environment

1.____

2. The author develops *context* so as to make it mean
    A. the nature of the child's immediate environment
    B. a complex rather than a simple home structure
    C. a multitude of past, present, and future forces
    D. internal as well as external influences

2.____

3. According to the author, the CRITICAL forces to be studied are those which
    A. are unconscious forces
    B. are conscious, unconscious, and subconscious forces
    C. cause the child to respond
    D. modify the child's interpersonal relationships

3.____

4. The author's point of view might BEST be labeled as
   A. environmentalist B. behaviorist
   C. psychobiosocial   D. gestaltist

4.____

5. The author maintains that the environment
   A. is relatively stable
   B. is in a constant state of flux
   C. shows periods of marked instability
   D. is more stable than unstable

5.____

6. From the above paragraph, it is to be inferred that the
   A. child's personality is mechanistically determined by the nature of the environment
   B. unique personality between the child and his environment shapes his personality
   C. child really shapes his own personality
   D. child's personality is more likely to be affected by than to affect the environment

6.____

7. By *structured behavior*, the author means
   A. conditioning of responses
   B. differentiated activity
   C. characteristic modes of reaction
   D. responses that have been modified by the developmental stream

7.____

8. The *patterns* to which the author refers are
   A. different for all children
   B. culturally determined mainly
   C. biologically determined mainly
   D. psychologically determined mainly

8.____

Questions 9-13.

DIRECTIONS: Questions 9 through 13 are to be answered on the basis of the following passage.

The Division of Child Guidance makes certain provisions for summer vacations for children receiving foster care. Foster parents wishing to take the child on a vacation within the United States must file Form CG-42 in duplicate at the office of the Division not later than 3 weeks prior to the starting date of the planned vacation. Such request must be approved in writing by the Social Investigator and the Assistant Supervisor. After the request has been approved, the original copy of Form CG-42 must be returned to the foster parents by the Social Investigator no later than 3 days prior to the planned starting date of the vacation. The city continues to pay the foster parents the standard rate for the child's care.
If the foster parents plan to take the child on a vacation outside the continental United States, Form CG-42 must be submitted in triplicate and must be received no later than 5 weeks prior to the starting date of the planned vacation. Such Form CG-42 for vacation outside the country must also be approved by the Case Supervisor. There will be no payment for time spent outside the United States.

When the approved original Form CG-42 is returned to the foster parents, it shall be accompanied by an original copy of Form CG-43. A duplicate copy of Form CG-43 shall be forwarded by the Case Supervisor to the Children's Accounts Section to stop payment for time expected to be spent outside the United States.

9. When a foster parent plans to take his foster child on a vacation trip, the Division of Child Guidance must receive Form
    A. CG-42 in triplicate no later than five weeks prior to the scheduled start of his vacation trip to Canada
    B. CG-42 in triplicate no later than three weeks prior to the scheduled start of his vacation trip to Mexico
    C. CG-43 in triplicate no later than three weeks prior to the scheduled start of the vacation trip to Arizona
    D. CG-43 in duplicate no later than five weeks prior to the scheduled start of his vacation trip regardless of location

10. The one of the following steps which is required in processing a request from a foster parent to take a child on a vacation trip is that the
    A. Case Supervisor send the original copy of Form CG-42 to the appropriate section in the case of a child who will spend all his vacation in a foreign country
    B. Children's Accounts Section receive the duplicate copy of Form CG-43 in the case of a child who will spend any part of his vacation in a foreign country
    C. Division of Child Guidance keep a permanent file of original copies of Form CG-43 to keep a control of all current vacation requests
    D. foster parents receive the triplicate copy of Form CG-42 from the Social Investigator in the case of a child who will spend part of his vacation in the United States

11. When a foster child spends an approved vacation with his foster father, payment for the child's care will be given to the foster father for
    A. none of the time if part of the vacation is spent in a foreign country
    B. that part of the vacation spent inside the United States but a reduced daily rate
    C. the entire period at a standard rate if the vacation is spent wholly in the United States
    D. the entire time regardless of whether or not it is spent in a foreign country

12. The Division of Child Guidance must notify a foster parent that his request to take his foster child on a vacation outside the country has been approved by sending him the approved _____ copy of Form CG-42 and _____ copy of CG-43.
    A. duplicate; duplicate   B. duplicate; original
    C. original; duplicate   D. original; original

13. On the basis of the above passage, children receiving foster care may be taken   13._____
    on a vacation trip by their foster parents to a location
    A. anywhere in the world with the written approval of the Social Investigator only
    B. of the foster parents' choosing but only with the written approval of both the Assistant Supervisor and Case Supervisor
    C. outside the United States but only with the written approval of the Social Investigator, Assistant Supervisor, and Case Supervisor
    D. within the United States with the written approval of the Case Supervisor only

Questions 14-18.

DIRECTIONS: Questions 14 through 18 are statements based on the following paragraphs. For each question, there are two statements.
Based on the information in the paragraphs, mark your answer:
A. if only statement I is correct;
B. if only statement II is correct;
C. if both statements are correct.
Mark your answer D if the excerpts do not contain sufficient evidence for concluding whether either or both statements are correct.

Almost 49,000 children were living in foster family homes or voluntary institutions in the state at the end of 2003. These were children whose parents or relatives were unable or unwilling to care for them in their own homes. The State Department of Social Services supervised the care of these children served under the auspices of 64 social services districts and more than 150 private agencies and institutions. Almost 8 out of every 1,000 children 18 years of age or younger were in care away from their homes at the end of 2003. This estimate does not include a substantial, but unknown, number of children living outside their own homes who were placed there by their parents, relatives, or others without the assistance of a social agency.

The number of children in care (dependent, neglected, and delinquent combined) was up by 4,500 or 10 percent over the 2000-2003 period. Both the city and state reported similar increases. In the comparable period, the state's child population (18 years or less) rose only three percent. Thus, the foster care rate showed a moderate increase to 7.7 per thousand in 2003 from 7.2 thousand in 2000. The city's foster care rate in 2003, at 10.5 per thousand, was almost twice that for upstate New York, 5.7 per thousand. (Excluding delinquent children from the total care in the state reduces the foster care rate per thousand to 7.2 in 2003 and the comparable 2000 figure to 6.7.)

Dependent and neglected children made up about 95 percent of the total number in foster family homes and voluntary institutions in the state at the end of 2003, as they did in 2000. Delinquent children sent into care (outside the state training school system) by the Family Court accounted for only 5 percent of the total. The number of delinquent children in care rose 5 percent, as an increase in the state, 28 percent, more than offset a 13 percent decline in the city. Delinquents comprised 4.9 percent of the total number of children in care upstate at the end of 2003 and 3.9 percent in the city.

14. I. There were 45,000 children in care away from their own homes over the 2000-2003 period.
    II. The percentage decline of delinquent children in care in the city in 2003 was offset by a greater increase in the rest of the state.

    14._____

15. I. The increase in delinquent care in the state from 2000 to 2003 cannot be determined from the data given.
    II. The state's foster care rate in 2003, exclusive of the city, was about one-half the rate for the city

    15._____

16. I. In 2000 and in 2003, the percentage of dependent and neglected children in foster family homes and voluntary institutions in the state was about the same
    II. In 2000, the number of dependent and neglected children in foster family homes and voluntary institutions in the state was 43,250

    16._____

17. I. The city's child population rose approximately three percent from 2000 to 2003.
    II. At the end of 2003, less than 1% of the children 18 years of age or younger were in care.

    17._____

18. I. Delinquents in the city comprised 4.4 percent of the total number of children in care in the city at the end of 2000.
    II. An unsubstantial number of children living outside their own homes were placed by their parents or relatives without the assistance of a social agency.

    18._____

Questions 19-25.

DIRECTIONS: Questions 19 through 25 are to be answered SOLELY on the basis of the information contained in the following paragraph. Each question consists of a statement. You are to indicate whether the statement is TRUE (T) or FALSE (F).

RESPONSIBILITY OF PARENTS

In a recent survey, ninety percent of the people interviewed felt that parents should be held responsible for the delinquency of their children. Forty-eight out of fifty states have laws holding parents criminally responsible for contributing to the delinquency of their children. It is generally accepted that parents are a major influence in the early moral development of their children. Yet, in spite of all this evidence, practical experience seems to prove that *punish the parents* laws are wrong. Legally, there is some question about the constitutionality of such laws. How far can one person be held responsible for the actions of another? Further, although there are many such laws, the fact remains that they are rarely used and where they are used, they fail in most cases to accomplish the end for which they were intended.

19. Nine out of ten of those interviewed held that parents should be responsible for the delinquency of their children.

    19._____

20. Forty-eight percent of the states have laws holding parents responsible for contributing to the delinquency of their children.   20.____

21. Most people feel that parents have little influence on the early moral development of their children.   21.____

22. Experience seems to indicate that laws holding parents responsible for children's delinquency are wrong.   22.____

23. There is no doubt that laws holding parents responsible for delinquency of their children are within the Constitution.   23.____

24. Laws holding parents responsible for delinquent children are not often enforced.   24.____

25. *Punish the parent* laws usually achieve their purpose.   25.____

KEY (CORRECT ANSWERS)

1.	A		11.	C
2.	D		12.	D
3.	D		13.	C
4.	C		14.	B
5.	B		15.	B
6.	B		16.	A
7.	C		17.	D
8.	A		18.	D
9.	A		19.	T
10.	B		20.	F

21.	F
22.	T
23.	F
24.	T
25.	F

TEST 2

DIRECTIONS: Each question or incomplete statement is followed by several suggested answers or completions. Select the one that BEST answers the question or completes the statement. *PRINT THE LETTER OF THE CORRECT ANSWER IN THE SPACE AT THE RIGHT.*

Questions 1-3.

DIRECTIONS: Questions 1 through 3 are to be answered SOLELY on the basis of the following passage.

    Undoubtedly, the ultimate solution to the housing problem of the hard-core slum does not lie in code enforcement, however defined. The only solution to that problem is demolition, clearance, and new construction. However, it is also clear that, even with government assistance, new construction is not keeping pace with the obsolescence and deterioration of the existing housing inventory of our cities. Add to this the facts of an increasing population and the continuing migration into metropolitan areas, as well as the demands for more and better housing that grow out of continuing economic prosperity and high employment, and some intimation may be gained of the dimensions of the problem of maintaining our housing supply so that it may begin to meet the need.

1. The one of the following that would be the MOST appropriate title for the above passage is
    A. PROBLEMS ASSOCIATED WITH MAINTAINING AN ADEQUATE HOUSING SUPPLY
    B. DEMOLITION AS A REMEDY FOR HOUSING PROBLEMS
    C. GOVERNMENT'S ESSENTIAL ROLE IN CODE ENFORCEMENT
    D. THE ULTIMATE SOLUTION TO THE HARD-CORE SLUM PROBLEM

1.____

2. According to the above passage, housing code enforcement is
    A. a way to encourage local initiative in urban renewal
    B. a valuable tool that has fallen into disuse
    C. inadequate as a solution to slum housing problems
    D. responsible for some of the housing problems since the code has not been adequately defined

2.____

3. The above passage makes it clear that the BASIC solution to the housing problem is to
    A. erect new buildings after demolition and site clearance
    B. discourage migration into the metropolitan area
    C. increase rents paid to landlords
    D. enforce the housing code strictly

3.____

Questions 4-5.

DIRECTIONS: Questions 4 and 5 are to be answered on the basis of the following passage.

Under common law, the tenant was obliged to continue to pay rent, at the risk of eviction, regardless of the condition of the premises. This obligation was based on the following established common law principles: first, that in the absence of express agreement, a lease does not contain any implied warrant of fitness or habitability; second, that the person in possession of premises has the obligation to repair and maintain them; and third, that a lease conveys an interest in real estate rather than binding one to a mutual obligation. Once having conveyed his property, the landlord's right to rent was unconditional. Thus, even if he made an express agreement to repair, the landlord's right to rent remained independent of his promise to repair. This doctrine, known as the *independence of covenant*, required the tenant to continue to pay rent or risk eviction, and to bring a separate action against the landlord for damages resulting from his breach of agreement to repair.

4. According to the above passage, common law provided that a lease would
   A. bar an ex parte action
   B. bind the parties thereto to a reciprocal obligation
   C. provide an absolute defense for breach of agreement
   D. transmit an interest in real property

5. According to the above passage, the *independence of covenants* required that the
   A. tenant continue to pay rent even for unfit housing
   B. landlord hold rents in escrow for aggrieved tenants
   C. landlord show valid cause for non-performance of lease requirements
   D. tenant surrender the demised premises in improved condition

Questions 6-11.

DIRECTIONS: Questions 6 through 11 are to be answered SOLELY on the basis of the information given in the following passage.

The City of X has set up a Maximum Base Rent Program for all rent-controlled apartments. The objective is to insure that the landlord will get a fair, but not excessive, profit on his building to stem the great tide of buildings being abandoned by their owners, and to encourage landlords to continue the upkeep of their property. The Maximum Base Rent Program permits the landlord to raise rents under carefully devised standards, while practically no raises in rents in this City were permitted under previous guidelines.

Under this plan, the City determines a Maximum Base Rent amount by means of a formula which takes into account the age of the building, the number of apartments, total rents received from the building, the amount of expenses, and labor costs. The Maximum Base Rent amount is to be recomputed every two year to allow for increases or decreases in building costs.

The Maximum Base Rent, which will allow the landlord to make a *fair return* on his investment, may not be collected immediately, however, since no rent increases over 7.5 percent will be permitted in any one year. The highest actual rent for each apartment during a given year will be called the Maximum Collectible Rent. This will be computed so that the increase over the present rent is not more than 7.5 percent ($7.50 on every $100.00). Sometimes, it may be less. Therefore, collectible rents will increase each year until the Maximum Base Rent is reached.

6. According to the above passage, the Maximum Base Rent is determined by the   6.____
   A. landlord
   B. Mayor
   C. Rent Commissioner
   D. City

7. Which of the following, according to the above passage, permits a *fair return*   7.____
   on the landlord's investment?
   The_____ Rent Program.
   A. Minimum Base
   B. Maximum Bass
   C. Minimum Collectible
   D. Maximum Collectible

8. It may be concluded from the above passage that the City of X hopes that   8.____
   insuring fair profits for landlords will be followed by
   A. good upkeep of apartment buildings
   B. decreased interest rates on home mortgages
   C. lower rents in the future
   D. a better formula for determining rents

9. According to the above passage, guidelines for determining rents previous to   9.____
   the Maximum Base Rent Program resulted in
   A. practically no raises in rents being made
   B. rent increases of approximately 10 percent a year
   C. a *fair return* to landlords from most rents
   D. landlords making too much money on their property

10. Based on the above passage, which is the MOST correct description of the   10.____
    kinds of facts that are taken into consideration when determining the Maximum
    Base Rent?
    Facts about
    A. labor costs and politics
    B. the landlord and labor costs
    C. the building and labor costs
    D. the building and the landlord

11. According to the above passage, the MAXIMUM annual increase in rent for   11.____
    a tenant in rent-controlled housing under the Maximum Base Rent Program is
    A. 7.5 percent each year for ten years
    B. 7.5 percent each year until the Maximum Base Rent is reached
    C. always under 7.5 percent a year
    D. $7.50 each year until it reaches $100.00

Questions 12-15.

DIRECTIONS: Questions 12 through 15 are to be answered SOLELY on the basis of the information contained in the following paragraph.

In all projects (except sites), when the Manager determines that a vacant apartment is to be permanently removed from the rent roll for any reason, e.g., the apartment has been converted to an office or community space, he shall notify the cashier by memorandum. The cashier shall enter the reduction in dwelling units in the Rent Control Book as of the first of the month following the date on which the apartment was vacated. He shall also prepare a reduction in Rent Roll (Form 105.046), the original of which is to be attached to the file copy of the Project Monthly Summary for the month during which the reduction is effective. Copies are to be sent to the Finance and Audit Department, Budget Section, and to the Chief of Insurance.

12. The purpose of the above paragraph is to provide for a procedure in handling
    A. the accounting for space occupied by offices and community centers
    B. apartments not rented as of the first of the month following the date on which the apartment was vacated
    C. vacant apartment temporarily used as office space
    D. vacant apartment permanently removed from the rent roll

13. The Rent Control Book is a control on the amount of monthly rents charged. According to the above paragraph, another function of the Rent Control Book is to indicate the
    A. number of offices and community spaces available in the project
    B. number of dwelling units in the project
    C. number of vacant apartments in the project
    D. rental loss for all offices and community spaces

14. In accordance with the above paragraph, the original of the Form 105.046 is to be
    A. sent to Central Office with the Project Monthly Summary
    B. kept in the project files with the project copy of the Project Monthly Summary
    C. sent to the Finance and Audit Department
    D. sent to the Chief of Insurance

15. The MOST likely reason for informing the Chief of Insurance of the removal of an apartment from the rent roll is to notify him
    A. to make adjustments in the insurance coverage
    B. of a future change in the address of the office or community space
    C. of a change in the project rent income
    D. of a possible increase in the number of project employees

Questions 16-20.

DIRECTIONS: Questions 16 through 20 are to be answered SOLELY on the basis of the information provided in the following passage.

It is the Housing Administration's policy that all tenants, whether new or transferring from one housing development to another, should be required to pay a standard security deposit of one month's rent based on the rent at the time of admission. There are, however, certain exceptions to this policy. Employees of the Administration shall not be required to pay a security deposit if they secure an apartment in an Administration development. Where the payment of a full security deposit may present a hardship to a tenant, the development's manager may allow a tenant to move into an apartment upon payment of only part of the security deposit. In such cases, however, the tenant must agree to gradually pay the balance of the deposit. If a tenant transfers from one apartment to another within the same project, the security deposit originally paid by the tenant for his former apartment will be acceptable for his new apartment, even if the rent in the new apartment is greater than the rent in the former one. Finally, tenants who receive public assistance need not pay a security deposit before moving into an apartment if the appropriate agency states, in writing, that it will pay the deposit. However, it is the responsibility of the development's manager to make certain that payment shall be received within one month of the date that the tenant moves into the apartment.

16. According to the above passage, when a tenant transfers from one apartment to another in the same development, the Housing Administration will
    A. accept the tenant's old security deposit as the security deposit for his new apartment regardless of the new apartment's rent
    B. refund the tenant's old security deposit and not require him to pay a new deposit
    C. keep the tenant's old security deposit and require him to pay a new deposit
    D. require the tenant to pay a new security deposit based on the difference between his old rent and his new rent

16.____

17. On the basis of the above passage, it is INCORRECT to state that a tenant who receives public assistance may move into an Administration development if
    A. he pays the appropriate security deposit
    B. the appropriate agency gives a written indication that it will pay the security deposit before the tenant moves in
    C. the appropriate agency states, by telephone, that it will pay the security deposit
    D. the appropriate agency writes the manager to indicate that the security deposit will be paid within one month but not less than two weeks from the date the tenant moves into the apartment

17.____

18. On the basis of the above passage, a tenant who transfers from an apartment in one development to an apartment in a different development will
    A. forfeit his old security deposit and be required to pay another deposit
    B. have his old security deposit refunded and not have to pay a new deposit
    C. pay the difference between his old security deposit and the new one
    D. have to pay a security deposit based on the new apartment's rent

18.____

19. The Housing Administration will NOT require payment of a security deposit if a tenant
    A. is an Administration employee
    B. is receiving public assistance
    C. claims that payment will present a hardship
    D. indicates, in writing, that he will be responsible for any damage done to his apartment

19.____

20. Of the following, the BEST title for the above passage is: 20.____
    A. SECURITY DEPOSITS – TRANSFERS
    B. SECURITY DEPOSITS – POLICY
    C. EXEMPTIONS AND EXCEPTIONS – SECURITY DEPOSITS
    D. AMOUNTS – SECURITY DEPOSITS

Questions 21-23.

DIRECTIONS: Questions 21 through 23 are to be answered SOLELY on the basis of the following paragraphs.

    In our program, we must continually strive to increase public good will and to maintain that good will which we have already established. It is important to remember in all your public contacts that to a good many people you are the Department. Don't take out any of your personal gripes on the public. When we must appeal to the public for cooperation, that is when any good will we have built up will come in handy. If the public has been given incorrect or incomplete help when seeking information or advice, or have received what they considered poor treatment in dealing with members of the Department, they will not provide a sympathetic audience when we direct our appeals to them.
    One of the Department activities in which there is considerable contact with the public is inspection. Any activity in this area poses special problems and makes your personal dealings with the individuals involved very important. You must bear in mind that you are dealing with people who are sensitive to the manner in which they are treated and you should guide yourself accordingly.
    Let us consider some of the aspects of the actual inspection of the premises:

    APPEARANCE: Your appearance will determine the initial impression made on anyone you deal with. It is often difficult to change a person's first impression, so try to make it a favorable one. Be neat and clean, show that you have taken some trouble to make a good appearance. Your appearance should form a part of a business-like attitude that should govern your inspection of any premises.

    APPROACH: Be courteous at all times. When you enter a building, immediately seek out the owner or occupant and ask his permission to inspect the premises. Ask him to accompany you on the inspection if he has the time, and explain to him the reasons why such inspections are made. Try to give him the feeling that this is a cooperative effort and that his part in this effort is appreciated. Do not make your approach on the basis that it is your legal right to inspect the premises; a coercive attitude tends to produce a hostile reaction.

21. Of the following, the BEST title for the subject covered in the above paragraphs is 21.____
    A. GOOD MANNERS   B. PUBLIC RELATIONS
    C. NEATNESS   D. INSPECTIONAL DUTIES

22. According to the above paragraph, the FIRST impression an inspector makes on the public is that of 22.____
    A. sympathy   B. courtesy
    C. cleanliness and dress   D. business attitude

23. According to the above paragraphs, if you want the public to cooperate with you, you must   23._____
    A. be available at all times
    B. be sure that any information you give them is correct
    C. make sure that their complaints are justified
    D. be stern in your dealings with landlords

Questions 24-25.

DIRECTIONS: Questions 24 and 25 are to be answered SOLELY on the basis of the following passage.

There is no simple solution for controlling crime and deviant behavior. There is no panacea for anti-social conduct. The sooner society gives up the search for a single control solution, the sooner society will be able to face up to the immensity of the task and the never-ending responsibility of our social structure.

24. Which of the following statements is BEST supported by the above passage?   24._____
    A. Although crime causation may be considered singular, crime control is many-faceted.
    B. When society faces up to the immensity of the crime problem, it will find a single solution to it.
    C. A multi-faceted approach to crime control is better than trying to find a single cause or cure.
    D. Our social structure is responsible for a continuing search for a simple solution to anti-social behavior.

25. The crime problem can be solved when   25._____
    A. it is realized that no solution exists
    B. the problem is specifically identified
    C. criminals are punished
    D. none of the above

KEY (CORRECT ANSWERS)

1.	A		11.	B
2.	C		12.	D
3.	A		13.	B
4.	D		14.	B
5.	A		15.	A
6.	D		16.	A
7.	B		17.	C
8.	A		18.	D
9.	A		19.	A
10.	C		20.	B

21. B
22. C
23. B
24. C
25. D

PREPARING WRITTEN MATERIAL

PARAGRAPH REARRANGEMENT
COMMENTARY

The sentences that follow are in scrambled order. You are to rearrange them in proper order and indicate the letter choice containing the correct answer at the space at the right.

Each group of sentences in this section is actually a paragraph presented in scrambled order. Each sentence in the group has a place in that paragraph; no sentence is to be left out. You are to read each group of sentences and decide upon the best order in which to put the sentences so as to form a well-organized paragraph.

The questions in this section measure the ability to solve a problem when all the facts relevant to its solution are not given.

More specifically, certain positions of responsibility and authority require the employee to discover connection between events sometimes, apparently, unrelated. In order to do this, the employee will find it necessary to correctly infer that unspecified events have probably occurred or are likely to occur. This ability becomes especially important when action must be taken on incomplete information.

Accordingly, these questions require competitors to choose among several suggested alternatives, each of which presents a different sequential arrangement of the events. Competitors must choose the MOST logical of the suggested sequences.

In order to do so, they may be required to draw on general knowledge to infer missing concepts or events that are essential to sequencing the given events. Competitors should be careful to infer only what is essential to the sequence. The plausibility of the wrong alternatives will always require the inclusion of unlikely events or of additional chains of events which are NOT essential to sequencing the given events.

It's very important to remember that you are looking for the best of the four possible choices, and that the best choice of all may not even be one of the answers you're given to choose from.

There is no one right way to solve these problems. Many people have found it helpful to first write out the order of the sentences, as they would have arranged them, on their scrap paper before looking at the possible answers. If their optimum answer is there, this can save them some time. If it isn't, this method can still give insight into solving the problem. Others find it most helpful to just go through each of the possible choices, contrasting each as they go along. You should use whatever method feels comfortable and works for you.

While most of these types of questions are not that difficult, we've added a higher percentage of the difficult type, just to give you more practice. Usually there are only one or two questions on this section that contain such subtle distinctions that you're unable to answer confidently. And you then may find yourself stuck deciding between two possible choices, neither of which you're sure about.

PREPARING WRITTEN MATERIAL
PARAGRAPH REARRANGEMENT
EXAMINATION SECTION
TEST 1

DIRECTIONS: The following groups of sentences need to be arranged in an order that makes sense. Select the letter preceding the sequence that represents the best sentence order. *PRINT THE LETTER OF THE CORRECT ANSWER IN THE SPACE AT THE RIGHT.*

1. I. The ostrich egg shell's legendary toughness makes it an excellent substitute for certain types of dishes or dinnerware, and in parts of Africa ostrich shells are cut and decorated for use as containers for water.
    II. Since prehistoric times, people have used the enormous egg of the ostrich as a part of their diet, a practice which has required much patience and hard work—to hard boil an ostrich egg takes about four hours.
    III. Opening the egg's shell, which is rock hard and nearly an inch thick, requires heavy tools, such as a saw or chisel; from inside, a baby ostrich must use a hornlike projection on its beak as a miniature pick-axe to escape from the egg.
    IV. The offspring of all higher-order animals originate from single egg cells that are carried by mothers, and most of these eggs are relatively small, often microscopic.
    V. The egg of the African ostrich, however, weighs a massive thirty pounds, making it the largest single cell on earth, and a common object of human curiosity and wonder.
    The BEST order is:
    A. V, IV, I, II, III   B. I, IV, V, III, II   C. IV, II, III, V, I   D. IV, V, II, III, I

1.____

2. I. Typically only a few feet high on the open sea, individual tsunami have been known to circle the entire globe two or three times if their progress is not interrupted, but are not usually dangerous until they approach the shallow water that surrounds land masses.
    II. Some of the most terrifying and damaging hazards caused by earthquakes are tsunami, which were once called "tidal waves"—a poorly chosen name, since these waves have nothing to do with tides.
    III. Then a wave, slowed by the sudden drag on the lower part of its moving water column, will pile upon itself, sometimes reaching a height of over 100 feet.
    IV. Tsunami (Japanese for "great harbor wave") are seismic waves that are caused by earthquakes near oceanic trenches, and once triggered, can travel up to 600 miles an hour on the open ocean.
    V. A land-shoaling tsunami is capable of extraordinary destruction; some tsunami have deposited large boats miles inland, washed out two-foot-thick seawalls, and scattered locomotive trains over long distances.
    The BEST order is:
    A. IV, I, III, II, V   B. I, III, IV, II, V   C. V, I, III, II, IV   D. II, IV, I, III, V

2.____

3. I. Soon, by the 1940s, jazz was the most popular type of music among American intellectuals and college students.
    II. In the early days of jazz, it was considered "lowdown" music, or music that was played only in rough, disreputable bars and taverns.
    III. However, jazz didn't take too long to develop from early ragtime melodies into more complex, sophisticated forms, such as Charlie Parker's "bebop" style of jazz.
    IV. After charismatic band leaders such as Duke Ellington and Count Basie brought jazz to a larger audience, and jazz continued to evolve into more complicated forms, white audiences began to accept and even to enjoy the new American art form.
    V. Many white Americans, who then dictated the tastes of society, were wary of music that was played almost exclusively in black clubs in the poorer sections of cities and towns.
    The BEST order is:
    A. V, IV, III, II, I   B. II, V, III, IV, I   C. IV, V, III, I, II   D. I, II, IV, III, V

4. I. Then, hanging in a windless place, the magnetized end of the needle would always point to the south.
    II. The needle could then be balanced on the rim of a cup, or the edge of a fingernail, but this balancing act was hard to maintain, and the needle often fell off.
    III. Other needles would point to the north, and it was important for any traveler finding his way with a compass to remember which kind of magnetized needle he was carrying.
    IV. To make some of the earliest compasses in recorded history, ancient Chinese "magicians" would rub a needle with a piece of magnetized iron called a lodestone.
    V. A more effective method of keeping the needle free to swing with its magnetic pull was to attach a strand of silk to the center of the needle with a tiny piece of wax.
    The BEST order is:
    A. IV, II, V, I, III   B. IV, III, V, II, I   C. IV, V, II, I, III   D. IV, I, III, V, II

5. I. The now-famous first mate of the *H.M.S. Bounty*, Fletcher Christian, founded one of the world's most peculiar civilizations in 1790.
    II. The men knew they had just committed a crime for which they could be hanged, so they set sail for Pitcairn, a remote, abandoned island in the far eastern region of the Polynesian archipelago, accompanied by twelve Polynesian women and six men.
    III. In a mutiny that has become legendary, Christian and the others forced Captain Bligh into a lifeboat and set him adrift off the coast of Tonga in April of 1789.
    IV. In early 1790, the *Bounty* landed at Pitcairn Island, where the men lived out the rest of their lives and founded an isolated community which to this day includes direct descendants of Christian and the other Crewmen.

V. The *Bounty*, commanded by Captain William Bligh, was in the middle of a global voyage, and Christian and his shipmates had come to the conclusion that Bligh was a reckless madman who would lead them to their deaths unless they took the ship from him.

The BEST order is:
A. IV, V, III, II, I B. I, III, V, II, IV C. I, V, III, II, IV D. III, I, V, IV, II

6.
I. But once the vines had been led to make orchids, the flowers had to be carefully hand-pollinated, because unpollinated orchids usually lasted less than a day, wilting and dropping off the vine before it had even become dark.
II. The Totonac farmers discovered that looping a vine back around once it reached a five-foot height on its host tree would cause the vine to flower.
III. Though they knew how to process the fruit pods and extract vanilla's flavoring agent, the Totonacs also knew that a wild vanilla vine did not produce abundant flowers or fruit.
IV. Wild vines climbed along the trunks and canopies of trees, and this constant upward growth diverted most of the vine's energy to making leaves instead of the orchid flowers that once pollinated, would produce the flavorful pods.
V. Hundreds of years before vanilla became a prized food flavoring in Europe and the Western World, the Totonac Indians of the Mexican Gulf Coast were skilled cultivators of the vanilla vine, whose fruit they literally worshipped as a goddess.

The BEST order is:
A. II, III, IV, I, V B. II, IV, III, I, V C. V, III, IV, II, I D. III, IV, I, II, V

7.
I. Once airborne, the spider is at the mercy of the air currents—usually the spider takes a brief journey, traveling close to the ground, but some have been found in air samples collected as high as 10,000 feet, or been reported landing on ships far out at sea.
II. Once a young spider has hatched, it must leave the environment into which it was born as quickly as possible, in order to avoid competing with its hundreds of brothers and sisters for food.
III. The silk rises into warm air currents, and as soon as the pull feels adequate the spider lets go and drifts up into the air, suspended from the silk strand in the same way that a person might parasail.
IV. To help young spiders do this, many species have adapted a practice known as "aerial dispersal," or, in common speech, "ballooning."
V. A spider that wants to leave its surroundings quickly will climb to the top of a grass system or twig, face into the wind, and aim its back end into the air, releasing a long stream of silk from the glands near the tip of its abdomen.

The BEST order is:
A. V, IV, II, III, I B. V, II, IV, I, III C. II, V, IV, III, I D. II, IV, V, III, I

8. I. For about a year, Tycho worked at a castle in Prague with a scientist named Johannes Kepler, but their association was cut short by another argument that drove Kepler out of the castle, to later develop, on his own, the theory of planetary orbits.
    II. Tycho found life without a nose embarrassing, so he made a new nose for himself out of silver, which reportedly remained glued to his face for the rest of his life.
    III. Tycho Brahe, the 17th-century Danish astronomer, is today more famous for his odd and arrogant personality than for any contribution he has made to our knowledge of the stars and planets.
    IV. Early in his career, as a student at Rostock University, Tycho got into an argument with another student about who was the better mathematician, and the two became so angry that the argument turned into a sword fight, during which Tycho's nose was sliced off.
    V. Later in his life, Tycho's arrogance may have kept him from playing a part in one of the greatest astronomical discoveries in history: the elliptical orbits of the solar system's planets.
    The BEST order is:
    A. I, IV, II, III, V   B. IV, II, III, V, I   C. IV, II, I, III, V   D. III, IV, II, V, I

9. I. The processionaries are so used to this routine that if a person picks up the end of a silk line and brings it back to the origin—creating a closed circle—the caterpillars may travel around and around for days, sometimes starving or freezing, without changing course.
    II. Rather than relying on sight or sound, the other caterpillars, who are lined up end-to-end behind the leader, travel to and from their nests by walking on this silk line, and each will reinforce it by laying down its own marking line as it passes over.
    III. In order to insure the safety of individuals, the processionary caterpillar nests in a tree with dozens of other caterpillars, and at night, when it is safest, they all leave together in search of food.
    IV. The processionary caterpillar of the European continent is a perfect illustration of how much some inspect species rely on instinct in their daily routines.
    V. As they leave their nests, the processionaries form a single-file line behind a leader who spins and lays out a silk line to mark the chosen path.
    The BEST order is:
    A. IV, III, V, II, I   B. III, V, IV, II, I   C. III, V, II, I, IV   D. IV, V, III, I, II

10. I. Often, the child is also given a handcrafted walker or push cart, to provide support for its first upright explorations.
    II. In traditional Indian families, a child's first steps are celebrated as a ceremonial event, rooted in ancient myth.
    III. These carts are often intricately designed to resemble the chariot of Krishna, an important figure in Indian mythology.
    IV. The sound of these anklet bells is intended to mimic the footsteps of the legendary child Rama, who is celebrated in devotional songs throughout India.

V. When the child's parents see that the child is ready to begin walking, they will fit it with specially designed ankle bracelets, adorned with gently ringing bells.

The BEST order is:
A. II, III, IV, I, V   B. II, V, III, I, IV   C. V, IV, I, III, II   D. V, III, II, I, IV

11. I. The settlers planted Osage oranges all across Middle America, and today long lines and rectangles of Osage orange trees can still be seen on the prairies, running along the former boundaries of farms that no longer exist.
II. After trying sod walls and water-filled ditches with no success, American farmers began to look for a plant that was adaptable to prairie weather, and that could be trimmed into a hedge that was "pig-tight, horse-high, and bull-strong."
III. The tree, so named because it bore a large (but inedible) fruit the size of an orange, was among the sturdiest and hardiest of American trees, and was prized among Native Americans for the strength and flexibility of bows which were made from its wood.
IV. The first people to practice agriculture on the American flatlands were faced with an important problem: what would they use to fence their land in a place that was almost entirely without trees or rocks?
V. Finally, an Illinois farmer brought the settlers a tree that was native to the land between the Red and Arkansas rivers, a tree called the Osage orange.

The BEST order is:
A. II, I, V, III, IV   B. I, II, III, IV, V   C. IV, II, V, III, I   D. IV, II, I, III, V

12. I. After about ten minutes of such spirited and complicated activity, the head dancer is free to make up his or her own movements while maintaining the interest of the New Year's crowd.
II. The dancer will then perform a series of leg kicks, while at the same time operating the lion's mouth with his own hand and moving the ears and eyes by means of a string which is attached to the dancer's own mouth.
III. The most difficult role of this dance belongs to the one who controls the lion's head; this person must lead all the other "parts" of the lion through the choreographed segments of the dance.
IV. The head dancer begins with a complex series of steps. alternately stepping forward with the head raised, and then retreating a few steps while lowering the head, a movement that is intended to create the impression that the lion is keeping a watchful eye for anything evil.
V. When performing a traditional Chinese New Year's lion dance, several performers must fit themselves inside a large lion costume and work together to enact different parts of the dance.

The BEST order is:
A. V, III, IV, II, I   B. III, IV, II, V, I   C. III, I, V, IV, II   D. IV, II, III, V, I

13. I. For many years the shell of the chambered nautilus was treasured in Europe for its beauty and intricacy, but collectors were unaware that they were in possession of the structure that marked a "missing link" in the evolution of marine mollusks.
   II. The nautilus, however, evolved a series of enclosed chambers in its shell, and invented a new use for the structure: the shell began to serve as a buoyancy device.
   III. Equipped with this new flotation device, the nautilus did not need the single, muscular foot of its predecessors, but instead developed flaps, tentacles, and a gentle form of jet propulsion that transformed it into the first mollusk able to take command of its own density and explore a three-dimensional world.
   IV. By pumping and adjusting air pressure into the chambers, the nautilus could spend the day resting on the bottom, and then rise toward the surface at night in search of food.
   V. The nautilus shell looks like a large snail shell, similar to those of its ancestors, who used their shells as protective coverings while they were anchored to the sea floor.
   The BEST order is:
   A. V, II, IV, I, III   B. V, I, II, III, IV   C. I, II, V, III, IV   D. I, V, II, IV, III

14. I. While France and England battled for control of the region, the Acadiens prospered on the fertile farmland, which was finally secured by England in 1713.
   II. Early in the 17th century, settlers from Western France founded a colony called Acadie in what is now the Canadian province of Nova Scotia.
   III. At this time, English officials feared the presence of spies among the Acadiens who might be loyal to their French homeland, and the Acadiens were deported to spots along the Atlantic and Caribbean shores of America.
   IV. The French settlers remained on this land, under English rule, for around forty years, until the beginning of the French and Indian War, another conflict between France and England.
   V. As the Acadien refugees drifted toward a final home in Southern Louisiana, neighbors shortened their name to "Cadien," and finally "Cajun," the name which the descendants of early Acadiens still call themselves.
   The BEST order is:
   A. I, IV, II, III, V   B. II, I, III, V, IV   C. II, I, IV, III, V   D. V, II, III, IV, I

15. I. Traditional households in the Eastern and Western regions of Africa serve two meals a day—one at around noon, and the other in the evening.
   II. The starch is then used in the way that Americans might use a spoon, to scoop up a portion of the main dish on the person's plate.
   III. The reason for the starch's inclusion in every meal has to do with taste as well as nutrition; African food can be very spicy, and the starch is known to cool the burning effect of the main dish.
   IV. When serving these meals, the main dish is usually served on individual plates, and the starch is served on a communal plate, from which diners break off a piece of bread or scoop rice or fufu in their fingers.

V. The typical meals usually consist of a thick stew or soup as the main course, and an accompanying starch—either bread, rice, or *fufu*, a starchy grain paste similar in consistency to mashed potatoes.
The BEST order is:
A. V, II, III, IV, I B. V, I, IV, III, II C. I, IV, V, III, II D. I, V, IV, II, III

16. I. In the early days of the American Midwest, Indiana settlers sometimes came together to hold an event called an apple peeling, where neighboring settlers gathered at the homestead of a host family to help prepare the hosts' apple crop for cooking, canning, and making apple butter.
II. At the beginning of the event, each peeler sat down in front of a ten- or twenty-gallon stone jar and was given a crock of apples and a paring knife.
III. Once a peeler had finished with a crock, another was placed next to him; if the peeler was an unmarried man, he kept a strict count of the number of apples he had peeled, because the winner was allowed to kiss the girl of his choice.
IV. The peeling usually ended by 9:30 in the evening, when the neighbors gathered in the host family's parlor for a dance social.
V. The apples were peeled, cored, and quartered, and then placed into the jar.
The BEST order is:
A. I, V, III, IV, II B. II, V, III, IV, I C. I, II, V, III, IV D. II, I, V, IV, III

16.____

17. I. If your pet turtle is a land turtle and is native to temperate climates, it will stop eating some time in October, which should be your cue to prepare the turtle for hibernation.
II. The box should then be covered with a wire screen, which will protect the turtle from any rodents or predators that might want to take advantage of a motionless and helpless animal.
III. When your turtle hasn't eaten for a while and appears ready to hibernate, it should be moved to its winter quarters, most likely a cellar or garage, where the temperature should range between 40° and 45°F.
IV. Instead of feeding the turtle, you should bathe it every day in warm water, to encourage the turtle to empty its intestines in preparation for its long winter sleep.
V. Here the turtle should be placed in a well-ventilated box whose bottom is covered with a moisture-absorbing layer of clay beads, and then filled three-fourths full with almost dry peat moss or wood chips, into which the turtle will burrow and sleep for several months.
The BEST order is:
A. I, IV, III, V, II B. III, IV, II, V, I C. III, II, IV, I, V D. IV, V, II, III, I

17.____

18. I. Once he has reached the nest, the hunter uses two sturdy bamboo poles like huge chopsticks to pull the next away from the mountainside, into a large basket that will be lowered to people waiting below.
II. The world's largest honeybees colonize the Nealese mountainsides, building honeycombs as large as a person on sheer rock faces that are often hundreds of feet high.

18.____

III. In the remote mountain country of Nepal, a small band of "honey hunters" carry out a tradition so ancient that 10,000 year-old drawings of the practice have been found in the caves of Nepal.
IV. To harvest the honey and beeswax from these combs, a honey hunter climbs above the nests, lowers a long bamboo-fiber ladder over the cliff, and then climbs down.
V. Throughout this dangerous practice, the hunter is stung repeatedly, and only the veterans, with skin that has been toughened over the years, are able to return from a hunt without the painful swelling caused by stings.

The BEST order is:
   A. II, IV, III, V, I   B. II, IV, I, V, III   C. V, III, II, IV, I   D. III, II, IV, I, V

19.
I. After the Romans left Britain, there were relentless attacks on the islands from the barbarian tribes of northern Germany—the Angles, Saxons, and Jutes.
II. As the empire weakened, Roman soldiers withdrew from Britain, leaving behind a country that continued to practice the Christian religion that had been introduced by the Romans.
III. Early Latin writings tell of a Christian warrior named Arturius (Arthur, in English) who led the British citizens to defeat these barbarian invades, and brought an extended period of peace to the lands of Britain.
IV. Long ago, the British Isles were part of the far-flung Roman Empire that extended across most of Europe and into Africa and Asia.
V. The romantic legend of King Arthur and his knights of the Round Table, one of the most popular and widespread stories of all time, appears to have some foundation in history.

The BEST order is:
   A. V, IV, III, II, I   B. V, IV, II, I, III   C. IV, V, II, III, I   D. IV, III, II, I, V

20.
I. The cylinder was allowed to cool until it could stand on its own, and then it was cut from the tube and split down the side with a single straight cut.
II. Nineteenth-century glassmakers, who had not yet discovered the glazier's modern techniques for making panes of glass, had to create a method for converting their blown gas into flat sheets.
III. The bubble was then pierced at the end to make a hole that opened up while the glassmaker gently spun it, creating a cylinder of glass.
IV. Turned on its side and laid on a conveyor belt, the cylinder was strengthened, or tempered, by being heated again and cooled very slowly, eventually flattening out into a single rectangular of glass.
V. To do this, the glassmaker dipped the end of a long tube into melted glass and blew into the other end of the tube, creating an expanding bubble of glass.

The BEST order is:
   A. II, V, III, IV, I   B. II, IV, V, III, I   C. III, V, II, IV, I   D. III, I, IV, V, II

21.
  I. The splints are almost always hidden, but horses are occasionally born whose splinted toes project from the leg on either side, just above the hoof.
  II. The second and fourth toes remained, but shrank to thin splints of bone that fused invisibly to the horse's leg bone.
  III. Horses are unique among mammals, having evolved feet that each end in what is essentially a single toe, capped by a large, sturdy hoof.
  IV. Julius Caesar, an emperor of ancient Rome, was said to have owned one of these three-toed horses, and considered it so special that he would not permit anyone else to ride it.
  V. Though the horse's earlier ancestors possessed the traditional mammalian set of five toes on each foot, the horse has retained only its third toe; its first and fifth toes disappeared completely as the horse evolved.

  The BEST order is:
  A. III, V, II, I, IV   B. V, III, II, IV, I   C. III, II, V, I, IV   D. V, II, III, I, IV

22.
  I. The new building materials—some of which are twenty feet long, and weigh nearly six tons—were transported to Pohnpei on rafts, and were brought into their present position by using hibiscus fiber ropes and leverage to move the stone columns upward along the inclined trunks of coconut palm trees.
  II. The ancestors built great fires to heat the stone, and then poured cool seawater on the columns, which caused the stone to contract and split along natural fracture lines.
  III. The now-abandoned enclave of Nan Madol, a group of 92 man-made islands off the shore of the Micronesian island of Pohnpei, is estimated to have been built around the year 500 A.D.
  IV. The islanders say their ancestors quarried stone columns from a nearby island, where large basalt columns were formed by the cooling of molten lava.
  V. The structures of Nan Madol are remarkable for the sheer size of some of the stone "longs" or columns that were used to create the walls of the offshore community, and today anthropologists can only rely on the information of existing local people for clues about how Nan Madol was built.

  The BEST order is:
  A. V, IV, III, II, I   B. V, III, I, IV, II   C. III, V, IV, II, I   D. III, I, IV, II, V

23.
  I. One of the most easily manipulated substances on earth, glass can be made into ceramic tiles that are composed of over 90% air.
  II. NASA's space shuttles are the first spacecraft ever designed to leave and re-enter the earth's atmosphere while remaining intact.
  III. These ceramic tiles are such effective insulators that when a tile emerges from the oven in which it was fired, it can be held safely in a person's hand by the edges while its interior still glows at a temperature well over 2000°F.
  IV. Eventually, the engineers were led to a material that is as old as our most ancient civilization.
  V. Because the temperature during atmospheric re-entry is so incredibly hot, it took NASA's engineers some time to find a substance capable of protecting the shuttles.

The BEST order is:
A. V, II, I, II, IV   B. II, V, IV, I, III   C. II, III, I, IV, V   D. V, IV, III, I, II

24. I. The secret to teaching any parakeet to talk is patience, and the understanding that when a bird talks," it is simply imitating what it hears, rather than putting ideas into words.
II. You should stay just out of sight of the bird and repeat the phrase you want it to learn, for at least fifteen minutes every morning and evening.
III. It is important to leave the bird without any words of encouragement or farewell; otherwise it might combine stray remarks or phrases, such as "Good night," with the phrase you are trying to teach it.
IV. For this reason, to train your bird to imitate your words you should keep it free of any distractions, especially other noises, while you are giving it "lesson."
V. After your repetition, you should quietly leave the bird alone for a while, to think over what it has just heard.
The BEST order is:
A. I, IV, II, V, III   B. I, II, IV, III, V   C. III, II, I, V, IV   D. III, I, V, IV, II

25. I. As a school approaches, fishermen from neighboring communities join their fishing boats together as a fleet, and string their gill nets together to make a huge fence that is held up by cork floats.
II. At a signal from the party leaders, or *nakura*, the family members pound the sides of the boats or beat the water with long poles, creating a sudden and deafening noise.
III. The fishermen work together to drag the trap into a half-circle that may reach 300 yards in diameter, and then the families move their boats to form the other half of the circle around the school of fish.
IV. The school of fish flee from the commotion into the awaiting trap, where a final wall of net is thrown over the open end of the half-circle, securing the day's haul.
V. Indonesian people from the area around the Sulu islands live on the sea, in floating villages made of lashed-together or stilted homes, and make much of their living by fishing their home waters for migrating schools of snapper, scad, and other fish.
The BEST order is:
A. I, V, III, IV, II   B. I, II, IV, III, V   C. V, I, II, III, IV   D. V, I, III, II, IV

KEY (CORRECT ANSWERS)

1.	D	11.	C
2.	D	12.	A
3.	B	13.	D
4.	A	14.	C
5.	C	15.	D
6.	C	16.	C
7.	D	17.	A
8.	D	18.	D
9.	A	19.	B
10.	B	20.	A

21. A
22. C
23. B
24. A
25. D

PREPARING WRITTEN MATERIAL
EXAMINATION SECTION
TEST 1

DIRECTIONS: Each short paragraph below is followed by four restatements or summaries of the information contained within it. Select the one that most completely and accurately states the information or opinion given in the paragraph. *PRINT THE LETTER OF THE CORRECT ANSWER IN THE SPACE AT THE RIGHT.*

1. Australia's koalas live solely on a diet of the leaves of the eucalyptus tree, a low-protein food that requires a koala to eat about three or four pounds of leaves a day. For most mammals, these strong-smelling leaves, saturated with toxins such as phenols and the oily compound known as cineole, are among the least digestible foods on the planet. However, the koala is equipped with a digestive system that is able to handle these toxins, trapping the tiniest leaf particles for as much as eight days while the sugars, proteins, and fats are extracted. 1.____
    A. Because eucalyptus leaves contain a large amount of toxins and oils, it takes a long time for koalas to digest them.
    B. Koalas have to eat three or four pounds of eucalyptus leaves a day, because the leaves are so poor in nutrients.
    C. Koalas have a unique digestive system that allows them to exist solely on a diet of eucalyptus leaves, which are generally toxic and inedible.
    D. The digestive system of the koala illustrates the unique evolutionary palette of the Australian continent.

2. Norway's special geopolitical position—it was the only NATO country to share a border with Russia—drove it to adopt much more cautious policies than other European countries during the Cold War. Its decision to join NATO led to strong protests from Russia, and in order to avoid provocation, Norway's foreign policy had to balance the need for ensuring defense capability with the need to keep tensions at the lowest possible level. Norway's low-tension "base policy" made clear the nation's refusal to allow foreign military forces on Norwegian territory as long as the country is not attacked or threatened with an attack. 2.____
    A. Norway's "base policy," in spite of its shared border with Russia, is the work of a pacifist nation that should serve as a model for foreign diplomacy everywhere.
    B. When Norway joined NATO, Russia feared a ground invasion over their shared border.
    C. The "base policy" of Norway is a perfect illustration on how much of Europe during the Cold War was a powder keg ready to explode at the slightest provocation.
    D. As the only member of the NATO alliance to border on Russia, Norway was forced to adopt a more conciliatory foreign policy than other members of the alliance.

3. During the women's suffrage movement of the early twentieth century, it was typical of many psychologists and anti-suffragists to automatically associate feminism with mental illness. In 1918, H.W. Frink wrote of feminists: "A certain proportion of at least the most militant suffragists are neurotics who in some instances are compensating for masculine trends, in others, are more or less successfully sublimating sadistic and homosexual ones." In the United States, anti-suffragists, finding comfort in psychology, concluded that suffragists all bordered hysteria and, thus, their arguments could not be taken seriously,
   A. The relationship between suffragism and feminism led many scientists to conclude that suffragists were afflicted with some kinds of mental illness.
   B. During the women's suffrage movement, anti-suffragists such as H.W. Frink tended to label women who fought for voting rights as mentally ill in order to dismiss their arguments.
   C. Responses to the women's suffrage movement are indicative of the tendency to label those who challenge the status quo as "Crazy" than to comfort their arguments.
   D. Most of the women who fought for suffrage during the early twentieth century were feminists who were mentally ill.

3.____

4. All of the earth's early plant life lived in the ocean, and most of these plants were concentrated in the shallow coastal waters, where the sun's energy could be easily absorbed. Because of the constant advance and retreat of tides in these regions, the plants—mostly algae—were repeatedly exposed to the atmosphere, and were forced to adapt to life out of water. It took millions of years before plant species had evolved that could survive out of the sea altogether, with stems that drew water from the ground, and a waxy covering to keep them from drying in the sun.
   A. After spending millions of years underwater, the earth's plants finally evolved ways of surviving on land.
   B. Most algaes today, because of evolutionary advances, are able to survive for extended periods of time out of water.
   C. Despite the fact that plants began as purely underwater organisms, they have always needed the sun's energy to survive.
   D. Land plants evolved from sea plants after millions of years in response to the gradual warming of the earth's atmosphere.

4.____

5. Because of the unique convergence of mild temperature and abundant rain (17 feet a year), British Columbia's temperate coastal rainforest is the most biologically productive ecosystem on earth. It's also an increasingly rare and vulnerable ecosystem: in its Holocene heyday, it covered only 0.2 percent of the earth's land surface. Today, logging and other development have consumed more than half this original range.
   A. The uniquely productive ecosystem of British Columbia's coastal rainforest has always been small, and has been reduced by human activity.
   B. Despite the fact that it is the most biologically productive ecosystem on earth, the coastal rainforest of British Columbia has been largely ignored by environmental activists.

5.____

3 (#1)

    C. The coastal rainforests of British Columbia have been nearly devastated by logging and other development.
    D. British Columbia's coastal rainforest originated during the Holocene Era, but has declined steadily ever since.

6. The Roman Empire, which ruled much of the Western world for hundreds of years, was led by an aristocratic class famous for its tendency to drink large amounts of wine. Recently, an American medical researcher theorized that this taste for wine was eventually what caused the decline and fall of the empire—not the drinking of the wine itself, but a gradual poisoning from the lead that was used to line and seal Roman wine casks. The researcher, Dr. S.C. Gilfillan, argues that this lead poisoning specifically affected members of the Empire's ruling class, because they were the Romans most likely to consume wine and other products, like preserved fruits, that were stored in lead-lined jars.
    A. The Roman aristocracy's taste for wine and dried fruits, according to one researcher, is a cautionary tale about the consequences of overindulgence.
    B. While the Roman Empire's ruling class suffered from widespread lead poisoning, most commoners remained in good health throughout the empire.
    C. One of the most far-fetched theories about the fall of the Roman Empire concerns itself with the lead used to line the wine casks and fruit jars of the ruling class.
    D. An American medical researcher has theorized that the fall of the Roman Empire was caused by slow poisoning from the lead used to line and seal Roman wine casks and fruit jars.

6._____

7. In the second century B.C., King Hiero of Syracuse called upon the renowned scientist, Archimedes, to find a way to see if his crown was made of pure gold or a combination of metals. Archimedes came upon the solution some time later, as he was entering a tub full of hot water and noticed that the weight of his body displaced a certain amount of water. Realizing that this same principle could be used on the crown, he forgot himself with excitement, jumping out of the tub and running naked through the town, yelling "Eureka! Eureka!"
    A. Archimedes, in making his famous discovery, unknowingly contributed the word "Eureka!" to the English vocabulary.
    B. The relative purity of gold can be determined by the amount of water it displaces when submerged.
    C. Archimedes, after discovering the solution to a scientific problem while stepping into his tub, became so excited that he ran through the town naked.
    D. The word "Eureka" has become a part of the English language because of an interesting story involving the ancient scientist, Archimedes.

7._____

8. In the nineteenth century most Americans had never heard of, let alone tasted, an abalone, the marine mollusk considered to be a delicacy by many Asians, and undisturbed abalone populations thrived all along the west coast. When the California Gold Rush of the 1840s and 1850s brought thousands of Asian

8._____

immigrants to America, many of these people began to harvest the dense beds of abalone that inhabited the state's intertidal zone. The Asian harvests eventually brought in annual catches of over 4 million pounds of abalone, and as a result, some county governments passed ordinances making it illegal to dive for abalone in waters less than twenty feet deep.
  A. The Asians who immigrated to California during the Gold Rush harvested so much abalone from intertidal waters that some governments were compelled to limit abalone diving.
  B. Abalone diving was unheard of in California before the Gold Rush, when many Asians immigrated to the state and began to harvest abalone from the intertidal zone.
  C. The extreme shortage of abalone in California's intertidal waters can be traced to the Asians who immigrated during the Gold Rush.
  D. The abalone of California's coastal waters generally live in waters less than twenty feet deep, where they are not protected by most county governments.

9. Maria Tallchief, the daughter of a full-blood Osage Indian from Oklahoma, was America's first internationally celebrated prima ballerina, rising to stardom at a time when classical American ballet was still struggling to gain international acceptance and acclaim. Her innovative interpretations of such classics as "Swan Lake" and "The Nutcracker" helped convince critics worldwide that American ballet was a force to be reckoned with, and her glamorous beauty helped popularize ballet in America at a time when very few people took it seriously.
  A. As ballet grew more popular in America, Maria Tallchief became a phenomenon in Europe, helping to secure a worldwide reputation for excellence for American ballet.
  B. Nobody in America took ballet seriously until the beautiful Maria Tallchief became an international star.
  C. With her beauty and technical innovations, Maria Tallchief gained unprecedented critical and popular success for American ballet.
  D. Before the success of Maria Tallchief, there were not many ballet dancers in the United States worth noticing.

9.____

10. Early in the Constitutional Convention of 1787, the idea of a two-tiered legislature was agreed upon by the framers of the Constitution. The final form of each of the resulting houses, however, was an issue that was debated openly, and which was finally resolved by the "great compromise" of the Constitutional Convention. While the House of Representatives was intended to be a large, politically sensitive body, the Senate was designed to be a moderating influence that would check the powers of the House.
  A. The framers of the Constitution could not agree on whether the nation's legislature should be bicameral, or two-tiered, at first, but after the "great compromise," they devised a House and Senate.
  B. The Constitutional Convention of 1787 ended with the "great compromise" that gave the nation its two-tiered legislature.

10.____

C. After much behind-the-scenes dealmaking, the two-tiered legislature of the United States was devised by the framers of the Constitution.
D. The framers of the Constitution, after some debate, decided on a two-tiered legislature made up of a House of Representatives and a Senate that was less susceptible to regional politics.

11. Although scientists have succeeded in creating robots able to process huge amounts of information, they are still struggling to create one whose reasoning ability matches that of a human baby. The main challenge facing these scientists is the difficulty of understanding and imitating the complex process of human perception and reasoning, which involve the ability to register and analyze even the smallest changes in the external environment, and then to act on those changes.   11._____
    A. Even the most sophisticated robot is unable to imitate innate human abilities such as learning to walk, converse, or perceive depth.
    B. Because of their inability to process large amounts of information, robots have yet to achieve even the most fundamental level of reasoning.
    C. Despite considerable technological advances, scientists have as yet been unable to produce a robot that can respond intelligently to changes in its environment.
    D. Because robots cannot automatically filter out all extraneous information and focus on the most important details of a given situation, they are unable to reason as well as humans.

12. Thor Heyerdahl, a Norwegian anthropologist, had long held the opinion that the Polynesian inhabitants of South Pacific islands such as Samoa, Tonga, and Fiji had actually been migrants from South America. To prove that this was possible, in 1947 Heyerdahl made a crude raft out of balsa wood, which he named after an Incan sun god, *Kon-Tiki*, and sailed from the coast of Peru to the islands east of Tahiti.   12._____
    A. Thor Heyerdahl's 1947 voyage on the *Kon-Tiki* proved that Polynesians probably had common ancestors in South America.
    B. While Thor Heyerdahl's *Kon-Tiki* voyage suggested a South American origin for Polynesians, most experts today believe the great migrations were launched from somewhere near Indonesia.
    C. To support the idea that Polynesians could have sailed from South America to the Pacific Islands, Thor Heyerdahl sailed the *Kon-Tiki* from Peru to Tahiti in 1947.
    D. Thor Heyerdahl's famous raft, the *Kon-Tiki*, was named for an Incan sun god, and was so well-made that it made it from Peru to Tahiti.

13. During the Age of Exploration, after thousands of miles of open sea, ships entered the bays of the Azore Islands, west of Portugal, with tattered sails, battered hulls, crewmen weakened from scurvy, and cargo holds laden with the treasure they had gained on their long trading journeys. Spanish, English, and Dutch warships prowled the waters around the Azores to protect this treasure, sometimes even sinking their own ships to keep it from falling into enemy   13._____

hands. During these fierce battles, many ships filled with treasure were sent to the ocean floor, where they still remain, preserved by the cold saltwater and centuries of rest.
- A. Although they are now sparsely populated, the Azore Islands were once a resting place for every ship returning from a long journey to the Americas.
- B. Many treasure hunters and archaeologists believe the sea floor around the Azores, a group of islands west of Portugal, still harbors some of the richest sunken treasure in the world.
- C. Economic competition between the European powers was so intense during the Age of Exploration that captains would rather sink their own ships rather than let their treasure fall into enemy hands.
- D. The rich history of the Azore Islands has deposited a large amount of sunken treasure in their surrounding waters.

14. The Whigs, a short-lived American political party, were wary of a domineering president, and many of them believed that the legislative branch should govern the nation. In particular, Whig leader Henry Clay often attempted to bully and belittle President John Tyler into submission. Tyler's resistance to Clay's high-handed tactics strengthened the office of the presidency, and in particular gave greater credibility to all later vice presidents who happened to succeed to the office.
    - A. While U.S. politics was at first dominated by the legislature, President John Tyler shifted the center of power to the presidency, while laying the groundwork for the downfall of the Whig Party.
    - B. President John Tyler, a failure by almost any other measure, can at least be credited with contributing to the strength of the presidency.
    - C. Henry Clay, who believed in a strong legislature, failed to win much influence over presidents who were not from the Whig Party.
    - D. President John Tyler, in resisting Henry Clay's bullying tactics, strengthened the U.S. presidency and lent credibility to the authority of vice presidential successors to the presidency.

15. By far the richest city on earth, Tokyo, Japan is also one of the most overcrowded; most of its people are only able to afford living in extremely small houses and apartments. In addition to cramped housing, Tokyo's overpopulation has created a commuter problem so grim that a corps of "pushers" has been hired by the city, to stand outside crowded commuter trains and help pack people inside. Problems such as these are so severe in Tokyo that there has been serious talk in recent years of moving Japan's capital elsewhere.
    - A. Despite the example of Tokyo, there is no evidence to suggest that economic wealth and overpopulation are related variables.
    - B. Tokyo's prosperity has led to such overcrowding that the country of Japan has recently begun to consider moving its capital to another location.
    - C. Despite being the richest city on earth, Tokyo, Japan is seriously overcrowded.
    - D. The small houses and apartments in Tokyo, along with its overcrowded transit system, are a perfect example of how economic wealth does not always improve a society's quality of life.

16. One of the greatest, and least publicized, legacies of Native American culture has been the worldwide cultivation of food staples through careful farming methods. Over centuries, tribes throughout North and South America domesticated the wild plants that have come to produce over half of the vegetables the world eats today. Corn, or maize, was first cultivated in the Mexican highlands almost seven thousand years ago, from a common wild grass called teosinte, and both potatoes and tomatoes were originally domesticated by the Peruvian Incas from native plants that still grow throughout Peru and Bolivia.

16._____

   A. Explorers of the Americas carried many native vegetables back to Europe, where they continued to adapt and flourish over the centuries.
   B. Today's common corn is a descendent of the wild Mexican teosinte plant, and potatoes and tomatoes were originally grown by the Incas.
   C. Without the agricultural knowledge and skill of early Native Americans, much of the world today would be in danger of famine.
   D. Foods that are today grown and eaten almost worldwide, such as corn, tomatoes, and potatoes, were first cultivated by the natives of North and South Americas.

17. America's transportation sector—95 percent of it driven by oil—consumes two-thirds of the petroleum used in the United States. With the 400 million cars now on the world's roads expected to grow to 1 billion by the year 2020, oil-foreign or not and other finite fossil-fuel resources will some day be conversation pieces for the nostalgic, rather than components of the nation's energy mix.

17._____

   A. In the future, most motor vehicles in the United States will be powered by an alternative energy source such as hydrogen or solar power.
   B. The continued growth of the oil-dependent transportation sector is outpacing the capacity of fossil-fuel energy resources.
   C. Our nation's dependence on foreign oil is a serious vulnerability that can only be corrected by increased domestic production.
   D. In the future, 1 billion cars across the world will be competing for oil and gasoline.

18. Althea Gibson, the first African-American to win the Wimbledon Tennis Championship, began her career by riding the subway out of her neighborhood in Harlem to 143rd Street, where she played paddle tennis against anyone who dared to challenge her. Since the Wimbledon tournament was played on grass, Gibson knew she would have to prepare herself by training on a surface that returned balls as quickly as a grass court. She found the solution to this problem in the gyms of Harlem, whose wood floors allowed her to perfect the rapid volley that helped her win two Wimbledon championships.

18._____

   A. Althea Gibson's tennis skills, including her famous volley, were developed in and around the inner-city neighborhood of Harlem.
   B. Althea Gibson had to leave her neighborhood to learn tennis, but to perfect her game, she had to return home to Harlem.
   C. Without the wood floors in the gyms of her Harlem neighborhood, Althea Gibson probably wouldn't have developed a volley that would help her win two Wimbledon tennis championships.

D. Although Althea Gibson achieved international fame as the first African-American to win the Wimbledon Tennis Championship, the path she followed to that championship was as unorthodox as the champion herself.

19. The greenhouse effect is a naturally occurring process that aids in heating the Earth's surface and atmosphere. It results from the fact that certain atmospheric gases, such as carbon dioxide, water vapor, and methane, are able to change the energy balance of the planet by being able to absorb longwave radiation from the Earth's surface. Without the greenhouse effect, life on this planet would probably not exist, as the average temperature of the Earth would be a chilly 5 degrees, rather than the present 59 degrees.

    A. The naturally-occurring greenhouse effect, by which atmospheric air is warmed, enables life to exist on earth.
    B. The greenhouse effect is a completely natural phenomenon that has nothing to do with human activity, and in fact it is beneficial to the planet's ecosystems.
    C. Human contributions to the increases in the greenhouse effect threaten life on Earth.
    D. In order for life to exist on Earth there must be some kind of greenhouse effect.

19.____

20. The religious and scientific communities have for centuries been at odds with each other, and held opposing viewpoints concerning the origin and nature of life. Progressive thinkers from both groups, however, claim that the two communities, in their ways of seeking answers to humanity's most important questions, share a common set of goals and procedures that would benefit greatly from a cooperative effort.

    A. Scientists and theologians will probably never agree on the origin and nature of life, though some progressive thinkers are trying to change the way the two communities talk about these issues.
    B. Though most scientists do not believe in God, progressive religious thinkers are continually trying to persuade them otherwise.
    C. Progressive religious and scientific thinkers have identified shared goals and questions that the two communities can work together to achieve and solve.
    D. Religious thinkers, who usually scorn such scientific theories as evolution, have begun to acknowledge the usefulness of science in answering important questions.

20.____

21. The administrations of Presidents Richard Nixon and Jimmy Carter oversaw an Export-Import Bank that was increasingly active in trade promotion, with expanding programs and lending authority. During this period, expenditures for program activities expanded to five times their 1969 rate, but the bank's net income dropped sharply—the low interest rates at which the bank financed its loan programs were lowering its profits.

    A. During the Nixon and Carter administrations, the budget of the Export-Import Bank grew to five times its 1969 expenditures.

21.____

B. Though the Export-Import Bank was very active during the Nixon and Carter administrations, its profits were reduced by its low interest rates.
C. Both the Nixon and Carter administrations demonstrated a lack of fiscal discipline that led to a declining net income at the Export-Import Bank.
D. Presidents Nixon and Carter both favored an activist Export-Import Bank, but while Nixon emphasized the function of trade promotion, Carter was more focused on making loans.

22. The Kombai and Korawai tribes of eastern Indonesia are known as the "tree people" for their custom of living in large tree houses, built as high as 150 feet above ground to avoid attacks from their enemies. These houses are built mostly from the fronds of the sago palm, a plant that also serves to produce one of the tree people's primary food sources—the larvae, or grub, of the scarab beetle. The tree people cultivate grubs by cutting a stretch of sago forest and then, after splitting and tying the palms together, leaving the palms to rot.   22.____
    A. The food-gathering methods of the Kombai and Korawai illustrate that deforestation is not a contemporary problem.
    B. The Kombai and Korawai people of eastern Indonesia relay on the sago palm for both food and housing.
    C. The Kombai and Korawai fears of enemy attacks have led them to build their trees high in the forest canopy
    D. Among the world's least-tamed native cultures are the Kombai and Korawai of Irian Jaya, the easternmost region of Indonesia.

23. It's no secret that corporate and federal information networks continue to deal with increasing bandwidth needs. The appetite for data—whether it's for internet access, file delivery, or the integration of digital voice applications—isn't likely to level off any time soon, and most information technology professionals allow that there is cause for concern. But emerging technologies for increasing raw bandwidth, accompanied by the streaming and maturing of transfer and switching protocols, are a good bet to accommodate the hunger for bandwidth, at least into the near future.   23.____
    A. There are two ways to decrease the demand for more bandwidth over computer networks: either increase the "raw" amount of bandwidth over an infrastructure, or devise more efficient transfer and switching protocols.
    B. Emerging technologies, aimed at the constantly increasing demand for bandwidth, are some day likely to result in virtually unlimited bandwidth for computer networks.
    C. Many different applications contribute to the demand for bandwidth over a computer network, and so the technologies that are devised to meet this demand must be many-faceted.
    D. While there is always a need for more bandwidth on large computer networks, newer technologies promise to increase the supply in the near term.

24. In the year 805, a Japanese Buddhist monk named Dengyo Daishi returned from his studies in China with some tea seeds, which he planted on a Japanese mountainside. In China, tea had long been the favorite drink of monks, because it helped them stay awake and attentive during their long periods of meditation, and Dengyo Daishi wanted to bring this practice to Japan. Over the centuries, tea-drinking would prove to be a custom that would influence nearly every aspect of Japanese culture, and Dengyo Daishi has long been considered a sort of saint among the Japanese.
    A. Because of the cultural similarities between China and Japan, it was only a matter of time before the ritual of tea-drinking made its way from the mainland to the island empire.
    B. Dengo Daishi, the first person to plant tea seeds in Japan, is revered among today's Japanese.
    C. The Japanese tea-drinking custom was begun in 805 by a Buddhist monk who brought tea seeds from China.
    D. Without the shared cultural traditions of Buddhism, it is unlikely that tea ever would have been imported from China to Japan.

25. Aztec women held a position in society that was far more respected than that of women in most Western civilizations of the time. For example, an Aztec wife was free to divorce a man who failed to provide for their children, or who was physically abusive, and once divorced, a woman was free to remarry whomever she chose. Perhaps the unusually high regard for Aztec women is best illustrated by the traditional Aztec religious belief that a special, elevated status in the afterlife was reserved for only two types of Aztec citizens-warriors who had died defending their tribe, and woman who had died during childbirth.
    A. The rights and privileges of Aztec women demonstrate that they were more respected by their societies than women of many cultures of the time.
    B. In the Aztec culture, women had the same rights and status as the most exalted men.
    C. Though the rights of Aztec women were still generally inferior to those of men, most Aztec women were granted a high degree of independence due to their service to the community.
    D. The relatively high position that Aztec women held in their society reveals the Aztec culture to be well ahead of its time.

KEY (CORRECT ANSWERS)

1.	C	11.	C
2.	D	12.	C
3.	B	13.	D
4.	A	14.	D
5.	A	15.	B
6.	D	16.	D
7.	C	17.	B
8.	A	18.	A
9.	C	19.	A
10.	D	20.	C

21.	B
22.	B
23.	D
24.	C
25.	A